Diet Recipe Book

Intermittent Fasting and Metabolism Foods for Weight Loss

Francis Harris and Rosie Townsend

Table of Contents

Introduction

If weight loss is your goal then you have a perfect start by choosing to go on the Intermittent Fasting Diet and the Metabolism Diet plans. Both diet plans are represented in this book.

Why Lose Weight?

Even if you feel good with the excessive weight, it probably won't last for long. Excessive weight gain can take a toll on the body. Here are the possible unpleasant side effects to being overweight: low energy level, high blood pressure, high cholesterol, high blood sugar, pain in bones and joints, muscle fatigue, and bad circulation. These conditions can lead to health concerns that are more serious such as cardiovascular disease, diabetes, and greater weight gain.

By losing weight, you lower your risks of the above health concerns considerably if not altogether. Going on a diet to lose weight is one of the safest and most effective methods of becoming healthier. But you must look at the dieting as a lifestyle change and not as a temporary fix. If you have gained weight then you obviously do not eat, as you should. If you go on a diet long enough to lose the weight and then go back to your old eating habits you will gain the weight back. You can do several things to make this a permanent lifestyle change. One is to break the junk food habit permanently. The other is to add exercise to your weekly routines.

Breaking the Junk Food Habit

A food eating habit is just like any other habit, and when it's junk food it's an intense bad habit. It is as real as a smoking or drinking habit. It takes the body about three weeks to wean completely from such bad habits. Sometimes the body needs help going through the weaning process. While you can stop eating (or smoking or drinking) you may have some bad withdrawal symptoms.

Junk food contains little to no nutrients. Eating it only adds fat to the body and makes the body more susceptible to the illnesses and physical conditions listed earlier. If you break the junk food habit, you will be more likely to stick on the diet. By breaking the junk food habit with a weaning process, you can do this painlessly. Stopping junk food without weaning may lead to unpleasant side effects such as headaches, moodiness, and intense food cravings, cravings for more junk food.

Start the weaning process by eating junk food just three times a day for five days. Do not eat it more than three. On the sixth day, eat it just twice a day for five days. On the eleventh day, eat it just once a day for five days. After this skip a day between eating junk food just once and do this for a week. After going through this process of elimination, you should be able to let go of the junk food fairly easily. If you still have issues with food cravings, skip two days for a week, then skip three days until you are eating junk food just once a week. Most people report they no longer crave it if they go through this process of elimination.

Physical Activity and Dieting

The body needs to be in motion in order to be healthy. The reason so many people struggle with issues of being overweight is due in part to a sedentary lifestyle. While we may be living very busy lifestyles we are often not physically active more so than we go from one chair to another. Technology is wonderful, but with its ever-increasing advances, we find more and more of us are stuck sitting in front of computers. This "butt in chair" leads us to sedentary lifestyles that add to our overweight issues.

In truth, it takes very little physical activity to help us be fit and healthy. It is not as if we must commit to several hour workouts every day at the gym to be fit. People mistakenly think that is what they must do and instead of doing something, they feel overwhelmed before they even start and do nothing. Follow some simple guidelines to be physically active and watch how it helps to lose the weight, have more energy, and feel better all the way around.

Physical activity just means you break a sweat by doing something physical for about a half an hour at a time. Ideally, you will want to exercise every other day for best results. Here are some good exercise suggestions: walking, running, jogging, swimming, bicycling, aerobics, weight lifting, gym circuit workout, dancing, playing sports such as baseball, softball, tennis, or soccer, and skating. Spend about five to ten minutes before and after the "workout" doing a warm up and cool down of stretches. Spend about half an hour working up to a sweat to make the exercise work. Do this at least every other day. This will help to reach your goals with weight loss.

Exercise helps to give you more energy, even though when you first start out you may not feel like doing it. It is something that once you get started it has a snowball effect where the energy builds. People often talk about feeling the runner's high after a good strenuous run. This happens because the body releases endorphins, a substance that helps to bring about a natural high. It helps to cure depression. Regular exercise helps to boost the metabolism, so the more you do it the more you will want to do it.

Disclaimer

Any new diet or exercise routine needs to be discussed with your health care provider first. All the advice in this book is for informational purposes only. This book is not meant to diagnose or treat any health condition. The recipes are nutritious and follow the intermittent fasting and metabolism boosting diet plans. As with any diet you will get out of it what you put into it. If you wish to succeed with the diet, stick with it and make a plan to change your lifestyle to eat healthier.

Section 1: Metabolism Diet

The metabolism diet is a diet in which addresses issues some people have who suffer from certain ailments that prevents them from dieting with other diet plans successfully. The bottom line is that unless you have enough energy to digest food properly, dieting will not help. On top of a sluggish digestive system, people who suffer from these issues also suffer from fatigue, lethargy, anxiety, weight gain, and the worse yet, craving bad carbohydrates. It also causes irritable and a low sex drive.

The metabolism diet helps a person to overcome the above issues, which may have prevented them from losing weight in the first place. By eating certain foods the body is able to build up energy, burn calories and fat and lose the weight.

Metabolism Diet Allowable Foods

The metabolism diet is very similar to the "low carb" diet, only not as extreme as the "low carb" diet. However, carbohydrates are very restricted. There are a few allowable carbs, but they fall in the category of being a "low carb" food, such as "low carb" breads and crackers. It is also a sugar free diet, so you are allowed "sugar free" foods; foods sweetened either naturally or with a sugar substitute. You are allowed all lean meats, and all "non starchy" vegetables. When going through the first who steps or phases of the diet you are supposed to limit the carbohydrate intake to just 5 grams every five hours. By step two, you can increase that to 20 grams every five hours. Then during maintenance, you are allowed 35 percent carbohydrate calories every five hours. It still requires you to think in terms of "low carb."

Metabolism Diet Avoided Foods List

Just like with the low carb diet, you are not allowed anything with sugar, which includes most "convenient" processed foods that contains enriched flours. In addition to the obvious sugary junk foods, these foods are on the avoid list: beans, bread, carrots, milk, parsnips, peas, pumpkin, rice, and yogurt. There are a few recipes below that call for minute amounts of milk, or a teaspoon or tablespoon of sugar, but it is dispersed through the dish so that there is not enough per serving to matter.

How the Metabolism Diet Helps with Weight Loss

By eating the foods on the allowable foods list, the body can shrink the fat cells, which helps to lose the weight. By stopping all the sugary foods, the pancreas is able to function better and not release too much insulin.

Other Foods Found to Boost Metabolism

Some foods that are on the "avoid" list for the official metabolism diet actually proves to help boost metabolism. Some fruits (which are on the avoid list) provides the body with energy to help burn more calories. You may want to include some of these in moderation. These foods are: grapefruit, oranges, and dairy products like yogurt and milk.

The Best Beverage for Boosting Metabolism

Of course, water is very good to drink, in fact vital to drink every day. Water helps to rid the body of toxins and helps to hydrate and keep the inside clean and clear. However, there is another beverage that is worthy of drinking every day and that is green tea. Instead of grabbing a cup of coffee in the morning, grab a cup of hot green tea. Or make a pitcher of iced green tea to drink with a meal. Green tea is a superfood because of the high amounts of nutrients found in it, in particular, anti-oxidants. It just stands to reason if you are consuming these vital nutrients your immune system will be in top shape. If your immune system is in best shape, you are able to keep from getting sick, and thus will more energy, a higher and faster metabolism. It all works together.

Advice to Help Facilitate Weight Loss While On the Metabolism Diet

A diet is only as good as you work it. If you only half way do the diet, you will not lose the weight you expect. If you cheat, it will put off weight loss or even reverse the loss and turn it into a gain. If you view a diet as a change of lifestyle, you will have greater success. Even if a diet has you going through different steps or phases, you do eventually reach a "maintenance" phase. This maintenance phase you should adopt as your change of dieting lifestyle.

What will happen if you follow the diet exactly? You will lose the weight. Your body determines the amount of weight you lose and the time it takes to lose the weight. Once you reach that weight loss goal, you must go on the maintenance. What will happen if you diet long enough to lose the weight then go back to your original eating habits? Your body will remember the way it was and it will go back to that, to whatever weight level you had. You will gain back every bit of the weight and fat, if you go back to the way you ate before the diet. This is why you see so many people go on diets, lose the weight and look great for a while, then turn around and gain it all back. It is an easy thing to do.

It is imperative that you take on the diet plan as a complete change of lifestyle. By doing this, you are insuring that fat and weight will stay off. When you go through the steps to lose the weight you are developing good eating habits. You are letting go of bad eating habits. While the craving may still be there, forever, you learn how to control it and avoid giving in to it in order to maintain your weight loss.

If you are serious about losing weight, you need to take it a step further and do more than just diet. Exercise is vital to weight and fat loss. Exercise if also very good for you. The more you exercise, the better you will feel in the long run. Exercise is like dieting, it is a lifestyle habit. Once you start it, you want to continue because of the benefits to your health.

Contrary to what you may think about if a little is good, then more is better, not so with exercise. You want to start slow and easy and increase it gradually. You may find it difficult in the beginning to exercise at all, and this is normal. Start small, walk around the block, or walk for 30 minutes. Do this every other day. See, it does not even have to be done daily; every other day will work just fine. If you start an exercise routine with your metabolism diet plan you will find the more into the diet you get the more energy you will have to exercise. You may discover that you will want to exercise more, to help burn off the energy.

When you add exercise to dieting, you help to make the weight loss happen faster. You will build muscles, which may add a little weight, but it is not fat and it helps to give you strength to do more exercises. Over time, you will have the energy to do more, which helps to keep the weight off.

Sample 5 Day Menu Plan

The metabolism diet uses a different approach than your standard "eat three big meals a day with snacks in between." The thought is by eating frequent smaller meals you will not be as hungry. You will feel less need for "snacking" and will be staying consistent on the right foods. Of course, you should discuss your meal plan with your health care provider, because you want to be sure that you are doing the best for your diet. The suggestions in this book are simply suggestions. The sample meal plan below does not take into consideration if you are in phase one or phase two or maintenance. It is merely showing you how to take the recipes from this book and plan 5 days of meals. Please adjust the meals to fit your diet plans.

The reason for eating smaller meals more frequently is to help raise the energy in the body or enhance the metabolism. If you eat every couple of hours (the right foods), it is as if you are giving your body the fuel it needs to move and be alert, focused, and feel good. By doing this you are causing the body to be constantly breaking down foods in the digestive system, and when doing this with healthy foods, it has a benefit of helping to raise the energy level.

Just because you are eating more often does not mean you eat the same large helpings you once did. If you are on this diet to lose weight, then you obviously had issues with portion control in the past. Now is the time to exercise control and eat less of everything. Instead of filling a dinner-sized plate with food, try eating on a dessert sized plate, and scaling back on the serving size.

Each meal should include a good balance of proteins and complex carbohydrates, in other words, meat and vegetables. By eating like this, you will be consuming less calories, which will help to shed the fat and the weight. If you can just avoid all junk food - food with sugar and processed flour you will essentially helping the body to boost the metabolism.

Day One

1 - Baked Omelet
2- Seasoned Quinoa
3 - Seafood Stew, salad, bread (from the bread recipes)
4 -Buffalo Wings

Day Two

1 - Mushroom Frittata with Asparagus
2- Collard Greens with Turkey
3 - Italian Meatballs, salad, bread (from the bread

recipes)

4 - Salsa and low carb chips

Day Three

1 - Pesto Eggs

2- Cheesy Spinach Casserole

3 - Spicy Marinated Grilled Shrimp, salad, bread (from the bread recipes)

4 -Cilantro Dipping Sauce and chicken

Day Four

1 - Spinach Quiche

2- Egg Drop Soup

3 - Roasted Turkey, salad, bread (from the bread recipes)

4 -Bakes Stuffed Mushrooms

Day Five

1 - Pancake Crepes

2- Broccoli and Cheese Casserole

3 - Parmesan Chicken, salad, bread (from the bread recipes)

4 - Cucumber Salad

Metabolism Diet Recipes

Breakfast Recipes

Baked Omelet

This is a crowd pleaser, perfect for large families or if you have guests, or even for a great different supper. Makes 8 servings.

What You'll Need:

1 can of mushrooms (12 oz., sliced)
1 can of black olives (6 oz., sliced)
1 dozen eggs
1 1/2 cups of cheddar cheese (shredded)
1 cup of turkey ham (chopped)
1/2 cup of skim milk
1/2 cup of onion (chopped)
1/4 cup of jalapeno peppers (sliced)
1/4 cup of butter
Salt and pepper

How to Make It:

Prep: Preheat the oven to 400 degrees Fahrenheit. Spray a 9x13 inch pan with cooking spray.

Place a skillet on medium heat and add the 1/4 cup of butter. Sauté the 1/2 cup of chopped onions. Next, create the layers by first adding the 1 1/2 cups of shredded cheddar cheese to the bottom of the sprayed 9x13 inch pan. Next layer the can of sliced mushrooms, can of sliced black olives, cup of chopped turkey ham, followed by the sautéed onions, and last the 1/4 cup of sliced jalapeno peppers. Crack the dozen eggs in a large bowl and beat with a whisk. Stir in the
1/2 cup of skim milk dashes of salt and pepper to taste. Pour the eggs over the food in the 9x13 pan, no stirring necessary. Place in the hot oven and bake until the top turns a slight golden brown and the eggs are set, about half an hour. Cool for a few minute before serving.

Mushroom Frittata with Asparagus

This is a delicious and filling breakfast made with mushrooms, eggs, asparagus, and Parmesan cheese. It is good enough to eat for supper too! Makes 6 servings.

What You'll Need:

6 eggs
1 1/4 cups of asparagus (fresh, trimmed to one inch pieces)
1 1/4 cups of mushrooms (fresh, sliced)
1/2 cup of mozzarella cheese (shredded)
3 tablespoons of olive oil
3 tablespoons of Parmesan cheese (grated)
1 tablespoon of water
1 tablespoon of butter
1 teaspoon of thyme (fresh chopped)

How to Make It:

Prep: Preheat the oven to 325 degrees Fahrenheit.

Set an oven safe skillet (cast iron works great) on the stove on medium heat. Add the 3 tablespoons of olive oil and the 1 1/4 cups of fresh trimmed asparagus, and cook until tender for ten minutes. Add the 1 1/4 cups of mushrooms stir and cook for an additional five minutes. Turn heat to low. In a bowl, crack the 6 eggs and beat, then add the 1 tablespoon of water and the teaspoon of fresh chopped thyme. Whisk together, then pour the eggs in the skillet, cover with a lid for five minutes. Remove from the stove, place in the preheated oven, and bake for an additional 12 minutes. Sprinkle the 1/2 cup of shredded mozzarella cheese and the 3 tablespoons of olive oil. Place back in the oven until the cheese melts and is hot and bubbly. Serve warm.

Pesto Eggs

This is another scrambled eggs recipe with a burst of flavor from your favorite pesto. Makes 4 servings.

What You'll Need:

4 eggs
1 cup of cheddar cheese (shredded)
4 tablespoons of canola oil
2 teaspoons of pesto
Salt and pepper

How to Make It:

Add the 4 tablespoons of canola oil to a skillet on medium heat. Crack the 4 eggs into a bowl and whisk in the cup of shredded cheddar cheese, and salt and pepper. Scramble until done. Stir in the 2 teaspoons of pesto and serve.

Spinach Quiche

A delicious wholesome and filling breakfast, this meal is good enough to be served any time of day. Makes 6 servings.

What You'll Need:

5 eggs
3 cups of Muenster cheese
1 1/4 cups of spinach (frozen, thawed, drained)
1/2 cup of onion (chopped)
1 tablespoon of canola oil
Salt and pepper to taste

How to Make It:

Prep: Preheat the oven to 350 degrees Fahrenheit. Spray a 9-inch pie pan with cooking spray.

Pour the tablespoon of canola oil into a skillet, set the heat on medium high. Add the 1/2 cup of chopped onions and sauté. Add the 1 1/4 cups of thawed and drained spinach and cook until semi-dry. In a separate bowl, crack the 5 eggs and beat with a whisk. Add the 3 cups of Muenster cheese and dashes of salt and pepper to taste. Stir in the cooked spinach and onions. Pour into the prepared 9-inch pie pan and bake for about half an hour, quiche is cooked when the eggs are set. Remove from oven and allow to cool for another 10 minutes.

Pancake Crepes

These delicious crepes can double as pancakes and tastes great with your favorite sugar free topping. Makes 6 servings.

What You'll Need:

2 eggs
1/3 cup of cream cheese (softened)
1 tablespoons of sugar free syrup
1 teaspoon of cinnamon (ground)
1 teaspoon of butter (and more)

How to Make It:

Beat the 2 eggs in a bowl, then gradually combine with the 1/3 cup of softened cream cheese. Combine until it is smooth, then stir in the tablespoon of sugar free syrup and the teaspoon of ground cinnamon. Place the butter in a skillet over medium heat. Pour about a 1/4 of a ladle of the batter onto the hot skillet and allow it to spread to coat the entire bottom. Cook for about 4 minutes, and then carefully flip to cook the other side for a minute. Do this until the entire pancake crepes are made, adding more butter as necessary to the skillet.

Scromlete

If you enjoy scrambled eggs and omelets you will love this quick and easy breakfast dish, the scromlete. Makes 4 servings.

What You'll Need:

5 eggs
1 cup of turkey ham (chopped)
1 cup of cheddar cheese (shredded)
1/2 cup of onion (chopped)
2 1/2 tablespoons of butter
2 tablespoons of milk
Salt and pepper
Garlic powder

How to Make It:

Crack the 5 eggs into a large bowl and beat with a whisk. Pour in the 2 tablespoons of milk and whisk. Add the 1 cup of turkey ham (chopped), 1 cup of cheddar cheese (shredded), 1/2 cup of onion (chopped), 2 tablespoons of milk, dashes of salt and pepper, and garlic powder to taste. Add the 2 1/2 tablespoons of butter to a skillet and heat to medium high. Pour in the eggs, and "scramble" until the eggs are cooked, about 10 minutes.

Serve immediately. Discard leftovers.

Breakfast Casserole

This casserole reminds us of staying at a cozy bed and breakfast inn, enjoying a tasty home cooked breakfast by the fireplace. Makes 4 servings.

What You'll Need:

4 eggs
1 cup of turkey ham (cubed)
3/4 cup of skim milk
1/2 cup of croutons *(Make them by lightly toasting and cubing the slices of one of the bread recipes in this book)*
1/2 cup of cheddar cheese (shredded)
1/4 cup of butter
1 teaspoon of dry mustard
1 teaspoon of onions (dried)

How to Make It:

First, put the 1/4 cup of butter into a glass 8x8 inch baking dish and microwave the butter until it melts. Stir in the 1/2 cup of croutons, and add the 1/2 cup of shredded cheddar cheese on top of the croutons. In a bowl, crack the 4 eggs and beat, then add the 3/4 cup of skim milk, the teaspoon of dry mustard and the teaspoon of dried onions. Pour the eggs into the 8x8 inch dish over the croutons and cheese. Cover with plastic wrap and refrigerate overnight (at least 8 hours). Place the casserole on the countertop while to oven is preheating to 375 degrees Fahrenheit. Place the casserole in the preheated oven and bake until the eggs are cooked, about 40 minutes. Allow cooling for 5 minutes on out of the oven before serving.

Bread Recipes

Flat Bread with Flax

This bread keeps you on the Metabolism Diet because it is low carb. Makes 8 servings.

What You'll Need:

1 1/2 cup of flax seed (meal)
1/2 cup of water
2 eggs
4 teaspoons of canola oil
2 teaspoons of baking powder
4 teaspoons of sucralose
1 teaspoon of salt

How to Make It:

Prep: Preheat the oven to 425 degrees Fahrenheit. Spaying a baking sheet with cooking spray.

Crack the 2 eggs into a bowl and beat. Add the 1/2 cup of water, 4 teaspoons of canola oil and the 4 teaspoons of sucralose and mix well. In a separate bowl, add the 1

1/2 cups of flax seed meal, 2 teaspoons of baking powder, and the teaspoon of salt and mix. Pour the egg batter into the dry ingredients stir to mix. Set aside for five minutes. Spread the batter onto the greased baking sheet into the desired diameter and size, about 1/4 to 1/2 inches thick. Bake for around 12 minutes. Remove from oven and cool for a few minutes before removing and serving. Store in a plastic bag, tightly closed, at room temperature.

Italian Spinach Bread

This is another version of a flat bread, that makes for a great addition with an Italian themed meal, or great as a sandwich bread. Makes 4 servings.

What You'll Need:

1 1/4 cups of spinach (frozen, chopped)
1/2 cup of Parmesan cheese (shredded)
4 eggs
1/2 teaspoon of Italian herbs (dried)
1/4 teaspoon of garlic (powder)
1 dash of cayenne pepper
Dashes of salt and pepper

How to Make It:

Prep: Preheat the oven to 350 degrees Fahrenheit. Spray a baking sheet with cooking spray.

First step, thaw the 1 1/4 cup of frozen chopped spinach and with hands squeeze the water from the leaves. Place the loose thawed chopped spinach leaves into a bowl. Beat the 4 eggs and add to the spinach, stirring to coat each piece of spinach. Combine the 1/2 cup of Parmesan cheese (shredded), 1/2 teaspoon of Italian herbs (dried), 1/4 teaspoon of garlic (powder), 1 dash of cayenne pepper, and dashes of salt and pepper with the spinach and eggs. Spread the spinach batter onto the prepared baking sheet to about a quarter inch thick. Bake in preheated oven until it turns a nice golden brown, or about twenty minutes. Using a spatula loosen from the baking sheet and set to the side to cool. Store the bread in a tightly closed plastic bag for a couple of days at room temperature. Discard uneaten bread after 2 days.

Peanut Butter Bread

This is actually a bread you can use for sandwiches, though it does not rise, it is more like a thick flat bread. Makes 12 one slice servings.

What You'll Need:

1 cup of peanut butter (creamy)
3 eggs
1 tablespoon of vinegar
2 teaspoons of sucralose
1/2 teaspoon of baking soda
1/4 teaspoon of salt

How to Make It:

Preheat oven to 350 degrees Fahrenheit. Spray a regular sized loaf pan with cooking spray.

Add the 3 eggs to a bowl and beat. Sir in the cup of creamy peanut butter. Add the 1 tablespoon of vinegar, 2 teaspoons of sucralose, 1/2 teaspoon of baking soda, and the 1/4 teaspoon of salt and combine. Pour batter into the prepared loaf pan. Cook until top turns a nice golden brown, about 35 minutes. Cool before removing from pan and slicing. Store in a plastic bag at room temperature.

Quick Soy Skillet Bread

This is a quick flat bread, fried on the stove in a skillet in olive oil. Makes 8 servings.

What You'll Need:

1 1/4 cups of soy flour (sifted)
1 cup of water (warm)
1/4 cup of olive oil
1/2 tablespoon of baking powder
1/2 tablespoon of onion (powder)
1/2 tablespoon of garlic (powder)
1/2 teaspoon of salt

How to Make It:

Stir with your hands and spoon or use an electric mixer with a dough attachment. In the bowl, add the 1 1/4 cups of sifted soy flour, 1/2 tablespoon of garlic powder, 1/2 tablespoon of onion powder, 1/2 tablespoon of baking powder, and the 1/2 teaspoon of salt and combine. Add the 1 cup of warm water, very slow, batter will be sticky. Preheat a skillet with the cup of olive oil. Rub soy flour on the hands and pick up the dough forming a four-inch diameter, 1/4 inch thick patty. Place in olive oil (carefully!) and "fry" until it turns a golden brown. Remove and drain on a paper towel until it is cool and dry.

Grain Free Bread

Here is a low carb recipe for a loaf of bread that is perfect for all the meals you need slices of bread. Makes 7 servings (2 slice servings).

What You'll Need:

3/4 cup of almond butter
1/4 cup of almond flour
1/4 cup of arrowroot
4 eggs
1 tablespoon of flax seed meal
1/2 teaspoon of baking powder
1/2 teaspoon of salt

How to Make It:

Prep: Preheat the oven to 350 degrees Fahrenheit and spray a regular sized loaf pan with cooking spray.

In a bowl, combine the 1/4 cup of almond flour with the 1/4 cup of arrowroot, tablespoon of flax seed meal, 1/2 teaspoon of baking powder, and the 1/2 teaspoon of salt. In a separate bowl crack and beat the 4 eggs first then combine with the 3/4 cup of almond butter. Slowly add the dry ingredients and stir until well mixed. Pour the batter into the prepared loaf pan and bake until golden brown, when a toothpick inserted in the middle comes out clean, about 22 minutes.

Cheese Zucchini Bread

This is a savory bread that makes a great side dish with meals, or make a sandwich using lean meat. Makes 10 servings.

What You'll Need:

1 1/2 cup of zucchini (shredded)
3/4 cup of almond flour
1/8 cup of cheddar cheese (shredded)
1/8 cup of Swiss cheese (shredded)
2 eggs
2 tablespoons of canola oil (plus 2 teaspoons)
1 tablespoon of onion (minced flakes)
1 tablespoon of Parmesan cheese (grated)
1 teaspoon of baking powder
1/8 teaspoon of garlic (powder)

How to Make It:

Prep: Preheat oven to 350 degrees Fahrenheit. Spray a 9 inch round pan with cooking spray. Makes 8 servings.

In a bowl, combine the 3/4 cup of almond flour with the teaspoon of baking powder. Set aside. In a separate bowl crack the 2 eggs and beat, then combine with the 1

1/2 cup of shredded zucchini, 2 tablespoons plus 2 teaspoons of canola oil, tablespoon of minced onion flakes, tablespoon of grated Parmesan cheese, and the 1/8 teaspoon of garlic powder. Gradually add the dry ingredients combining until smooth. Pour into the prepared 9 inch round pan. Sprinkle the top with the 1/8 cup of shredded cheddar cheese and the 1/8 cup of shredded Swiss cheese. Bake until an inserted toothpick in the middle comes out clean, about 40 minutes. Best if served warm. Tastes great toasted as well.

Snacks, Desserts and Appetizer Recipes

Jalapeno Poppers

These are always a favorite at parties and gatherings. Makes 2 dozen.

What You'll Need:

12 jalapeno peppers (cut lengthwise, all insides scraped out)
2 eggs
1 cup of bread crumbs (fine crumbs, dried Flat Bread with Flax recipe)
3/4 cup of Monterey Jack cheese(shredded)
3/4 cup of mozzarella cheese (shredded)
3/4 cup of cream cheese (softened)
1/2 cup of quinoa flour
2 tablespoons of milk
2 tablespoons plus 2 teaspoons of Creole seasoning
1/2 teaspoon of cayenne pepper
1/2 teaspoon of cumin (ground)

How to Make It:

Prep: Preheat oven to 350 degrees Fahrenheit. Spray a baking sheet with cooking spray.

Add the 3/4 cup of softened cream cheese to a bowl with the shredded 3/4 cups of Monterey Jack cheese and mozzarella cheese. Combine with the 1/2 teaspoons of ground cumin and cayenne pepper. In a separate bowl, crack and beat the 2 eggs with the 2 tablespoons of milk and the 2 teaspoons of Creole seasoning. In a shallow dish, combine the cup of fine dried breadcrumbs with a tablespoon and a half of the Creole seasoning. In another bowl, combine the 1/2 cup of quinoa flour with the remaining 1/2 tablespoon of Creole seasoning. Set up an assembly line, by first taking a jalapeno half, spoon some of the cheese mixture into the center. Next roll it through the quinoa flour mixture, then dip it in the egg mixture, then roll it in the dry bread crumb mixture, and set on the baking sheet, with the cheese side facing up. Do this with all 24 jalapeno halves. Bake in hot oven for half an hour, until the peppers are a golden crispy brown.

Buffalo Wings

These make for an excellent appetizer or snack, but can also serve as the main course of a supper too. Makes 8 servings

What You'll Need:

24 chicken wings (cut in half)
4 cups of canola oil
5 tablespoons of hot pepper sauce
4 tablespoons of butter
1 tablespoon of vinegar (white distilled)
Salt and pepper

How to Make It:

Heat the 4 cups of canola oil in a deep fryer to reach 375 degrees Fahrenheit. Gently fry the 24 halved chicken wings, takes about 10 minutes. Drain on a plate of paper towels. Meanwhile, in a skillet on the stove on low heat add the 4 tablespoons of butter and melt. Add dashes of salt and pepper and mix in the 5 tablespoons of hot pepper sauce and the tablespoon of white distilled vinegar. Add the fried chicken wings and allow simmering for a few minutes. Best if served immediately.

Salsa

A delicious salsa goes well with so many foods, enjoy as a snack with low carb chips, or as a garnish with meats and vegetables. Makes 16 servings.

What You'll Need:

2 cans of tomatoes (14.5 oz. each, stewed undrained)
1/4 cup of onion (fine diced)
1/4 cup of green chilies (sliced)
3 tablespoons of cilantro (fresh chopped)
1 tablespoon of lime juice
1 teaspoon of garlic (minced)
1 teaspoon of salt

How to Make It:

Add the 2 cans of tomatoes (14.5 oz. each, stewed undrained), 1/4 cup of onion (fine diced), 1/4 cup of green chilies (sliced), 3 tablespoons of cilantro (fresh chopped), 1 tablespoon of lime juice, 1 teaspoon of garlic (minced), and 1 teaspoon of salt into a blender or food processor and chop to blend. Do not blend until smooth, leave it a bit chunky.

Artichoke Spinach Dip

This is a delicious favorite at parties and gatherings or just as a fun addition with supper or a snack. Makes up to 12 servings.

What You'll Need:

1 can of artichoke hearts (14 oz., drained, chopped)
1 jar of Alfredo-style pasta sauce (10 oz.)
1 1/4 cups of spinach (frozen, thawed, drained)
1 cup of mozzarella cheese (shredded)
1/2 cup of cream cheese (softened)
1/3 cup of Parmesan cheese (grated)
2 teaspoons of garlic (minced)

How to Make It:

Prep: Preheat oven to 350 degrees Fahrenheit.

Mix the 1 can of artichoke hearts (14 oz., drained, chopped), 1 jar of Alfredo-style pasta sauce (10 oz.), 1 1/4 cups of spinach (frozen, thawed, drained), 1 cup of mozzarella cheese (shredded), 1/2 cup of cream cheese (softened), 1/3 cup of Parmesan cheese (grated), and 2 teaspoons of garlic (minced) in a bowl, then pour into an 8x8 inch baking dish and bake for half an hour. Allow to cool for a few minutes, best if served warm.

Cilantro Dipping Sauce

This is a delicious and savory dipping sauce, perfect for dipping chicken or raw vegetables. Makes 4 servings.

What You'll Need:

1 package of cream cheese (8 oz., softened to room temperature)
1 can of tomatillo salsa (7 oz., can or jar)
3/4 cup of cilantro (fresh chopped)
1 tablespoon of sour cream
1 tablespoon of lime juice
2 teaspoons of garlic (powder)
1 teaspoon of pepper
1 teaspoon of celery salt
1/2 teaspoon of cumin (ground)

How to Make It:

Add the 1 package of cream cheese (8 oz., softened to room temperature), 1 can of tomatillo salsa (7 oz., can or jar), 3/4 cup of cilantro (fresh chopped), 1 tablespoon of sour cream, 1 tablespoon of lime juice, 2 teaspoons of garlic (powder), 1 teaspoon of pepper, 1 teaspoon of celery salt, and 1/2 teaspoon of cumin (ground) in a blender or food processor to combine. Pour in a serving bowl, cover and refrigerate for at least 30 minutes before serving.

Cheese Ball

This is a wonderful low carb dish, best served on a slice of bread from one of the bread recipes, or a low carb cracker. Makes a large cheese ball.

What You'll Need:

2 packages of cream cheese (8 ounces, softened to room temperature)
1 package of Ranch dressing mix
3 1/2 cups of cheddar cheese (sharp)
2 cups of pecans (chopped)
2 tablespoons of chives (dried)

How to Make It:

Add the 2 packages of cream cheese to a bowl, mash with a fork, then add the 1 package of Ranch dressing mix, 3 1/2 cups of cheddar cheese (sharp), and the 2 tablespoons of chives (dried) and continue to mix with a fork. Shape into a large ball, roll in the 2 cups of pecans. Cover and let sit in the refrigerator for at least half an hour before serving, longer or overnight is better

Homemade Ranch Dressing

Ranch dressing goes with so many snack foods; it just had to go in this category. Enjoy on a salad, with chicken, or as a vegetable dip. Makes a batch of 1 1/2 cups.

What You'll Need:

1 cup of mayonnaise
1/2 cup of sour cream
1/2 teaspoon of chives (dried)
1/2 teaspoon of dill weed (dried)
1/2 teaspoon of parsley (dried)
1/4 teaspoon of garlic (powder)
1/4 teaspoon of onion (powder)
1/8 teaspoon of salt
1/8 teaspoon of black pepper (ground)

How to Make It:

Using a whisk in a bowl, combine the 1 cup of mayonnaise, 1/2 cup of sour cream, 1/2 teaspoon of chives (dried), 1/2 teaspoon of dill weed (dried), 1/2 teaspoon of parsley (dried), 1/4 teaspoon of garlic (powder), 1/4 teaspoon of onion (powder), 1/8 teaspoon of salt, and 1/8 teaspoon of black pepper (ground). Cover the bowl with a lid or plastic wrap and refrigerate for at least half an hour before serving.

Baked Stuffed Mushrooms

This is a delicious and filling appetizer, perfect for a party or a nice addition to a big meal. Makes 12 servings.

What You'll Need:

Dozen large mushrooms
1 cup of cream cheese (softened to room temperature)
1/4 cup of Parmesan cheese (grated)
1 tablespoon of canola oil
1 tablespoon of garlic (minced)
1/4 teaspoon of cayenne pepper (ground)
1/4 teaspoon of onion powder
1/4 teaspoon of pepper (black)

How to Make It:

Prep: Preheat the oven to 350 degrees Fahrenheit. Spray a baking sheet with cooking spray.

Using a damp cloth, clean the dozen large mushrooms, and then cut of the end of the stems and discard, then cut off the whole stems and chop the stems fine. Add the tablespoon of canola oil to a skillet and turn to medium heat. Add the fine chopped mushroom stems to the hot oil along with the tablespoon of minced garlic and stir and fry until the mushrooms are dry. Set aside off the burner to cool. Next, add the cup of softened cream cheese, 1/4 cup of grated Parmesan cheese, 1/4 teaspoon of cayenne pepper (ground), 1/4 teaspoon of onion powder, and 1/4 teaspoon of pepper (black) and stir till combined. Spoon evenly into each mushroom cap, arranging the caps on the prepared baking sheet. Bake until liquid appears under the mushrooms, about 20 minutes. Cool for a couple of minutes and serve.

Guacamole

Everyone loves guacamole with a delicious Mexican dish; it goes well with so many foods. Makes 4 servings.

What You'll Need:

3 avocados (peeled, pitted, chunked and mashed)
1/2 cup of onions (diced)
1/3 cup of tomatoes (small chopped)
3 tablespoons of cilantro (fresh chopped)
2 tablespoons of lime juice
1 teaspoon of garlic (minced)
1 teaspoon of salt
1 pinch of cayenne pepper (ground)

How to Make It:

Add 3 avocados (peeled, pitted, chunked and mashed), 1/2 cup of onions (diced), 1/3 cup of tomatoes (small chopped), 3 tablespoons of cilantro (fresh chopped), 2 tablespoons of lime juice, 1 teaspoon of garlic (minced), 1 teaspoon of salt, and 1 pinch of cayenne pepper (ground) to a bowl and combine. Set in refrigerate for at least an hour. Store in refrigerator, serve cold.

Cucumber Salad

Mediterranean cooking inspires this cool salad.

What You'll Need:

4 1/2 cups of cucumbers (sliced, seeded)
3 cups of tomatoes (diced)
1 1/2 cups of feta cheese (crumbled)
1 cup of black olives (pitted, sliced)
1/3 cup of sun-dried tomatoes (drained, keep oil)
1/4 cup of onion (sliced)

How to Make It:

Toss 4 1/2 cups of cucumbers (sliced, seeded), 3 cups of tomatoes (diced), 1 1/2 cups of feta cheese (crumbled), 1 cup of black olives (pitted, sliced), 1/3 cup of sun-dried tomatoes (drained, keep oil), and 1/4 cup of onion (sliced) in a large salad serving bowl. Drizzle the oil from the sun-dried tomatoes over the salad. Serve immediately, or store in the refrigerator.

Sugar Free Cherry Cookies

These cookies tastes like they have real sugar, only they do not. Makes 48 cookies.

What You'll Need:

1 cup of sucralose
6 egg whites (room temperature)
1 1/2 teaspoons of sugar-free gelatin mix (cherry)
1/4 teaspoon of cream of tartar
1/4 teaspoon of salt

How to Make It:

Prep: Preheat the oven to 250 degrees Fahrenheit. Place parchment paper over 2 cookie sheets.

Use a cake decorating bag with a star tip (or use a plastic bag, corner cut, with a star tip). Mix the cup of sucralose with the 1 1/2 teaspoons of cherry flavored sugar-free gelatin mix. In a separate bowl, add the 6 room temperature egg whites, 1/4 teaspoon of cream of tartar, and the 1/4 teaspoon of salt. Using an electric beater, beat the egg whites until they form stiff white peaks. Gradually add the sucralose and gelatin powder, a little at a time while running the beater. Put the mixture into the cake decorator bag (or plastic bag) and squeeze out heaping tablespoon sized "balls" onto the cooking sheets, making them decorative shape if desired. Make 48 cookies. Bake for around 90 minutes, careful to keep the oven closed the entire time. Turn the oven off, and let the cookies sit for another 10 minutes before removing and serving or storing in a sealed container.

Side Dish Recipes

Broccoli and Cheese Casserole

This is a perfect side dish with chicken or beef. Makes 8 servings.

What You'll Need:

1 can of cream of mushroom soup (10.75 oz.)
9 1/3 cups of broccoli (frozen chopped florets)
2 cups of cheddar cheese (sharp, shredded)
1 cup of mayonnaise
1/4 cup of onions (fine chopped)
1 egg
Salt and pepper
Paprika

How to Make It:

Prep: Preheat the oven to 350 degrees Fahrenheit. Spray a 9x13 inch baking dish with cooking spray.

Beat an egg in a bowl and then add the 10.75 oz. can of cream of mushroom soup and 1 cup of mayonnaise, and stir with a whisk. Stir in the 1/4 cup of fine chopped onions. Add the 9 1/3 cups of frozen broccoli florets to a large bowl. Pour the soup mixture over the frozen broccoli and toss to mix throughout. Add the 2 cups of shredded sharp cheddar cheese and mix. Pour the broccoli mixture into the prepared 9x13 inch baking dish. Sprinkle with dashes of salt, pepper, and paprika to taste. Bake for around 52 minutes, until hot and bubbly.

Egg Drop Soup

This delicious soup is great as a lunch too. Makes 4 servings.

What You'll Need:

4 cups of chicken stock (divided into 3 1/4 cups and 3/4 cup)
2 eggs
1 extra egg yolk
2 tablespoons of chives (fresh chopped)
1 1/2 tablespoons of cornstarch
1/4 teaspoon of salt
1/8 teaspoon of ginger (ground)

How to Make It:

Add 3 1/4 cups of chicken stock to a large saucepan on high heat. Add the 2 tablespoons of fresh chopped chives, 1/4 teaspoon of salt, and 1/8 teaspoon of ground ginger and stir until it boils. Meanwhile, add the 1 1/2 tablespoons of cornstarch to the remaining 3/4 cup of chicken stock stir and set aside. In a separate bowl, crack the 2 eggs and add the extra egg yolk and stir with a whisk. Stir the boiling soup and begin to drop the eggs, a little at a time, to allow them to separate and cook. Once all the eggs are added, stir in the 3/4 cup of chicken stock and cornstarch. Stir until it reaches the desired consistency, cut the heat, cool for a few minutes and serve.

Fried Tahini Cauliflower

This is a delicious side dish of fried cauliflower dipped in a tasty tahini sauce. Makes 6 servings.

What You'll Need:

1 head of cauliflower (chopped)
3 cups of canola oil
1/3 cup of tahini
1/3 cup of water
1/4 cup of lemon juice (a little less than 1/4 cup)
1 tablespoon of parsley (fresh chopped)
1 teaspoon of garlic (minced)
Salt and pepper

How to Make It:

Add the 1/3 cup of tahini with the 1/3 cup of water, a little less than 1/4 cup of lemon juice, tablespoon of fresh chopped parsley, teaspoon of minced garlic, and salt and pepper to taste, mix well with a whisk. Add more water if it is too thick. Pour the 3 cups of canola oil (or more if needed) in a deep skillet and heat to medium high. Fry the cauliflower pieces by adding just enough for a single layer in the skillet until they turn a light golden brown, just under 10 minutes. Continue until the entire head is fried. Drain on paper towels on a wire rack. Serve warm with the sauce.

Collard Greens with Turkey

This delicious side dish is as nutritious as it is tasty. Makes 10 servings.

What You'll Need:

1 turkey drumstick (smoked)
7 1/2 cups of collard greens (about 5 bunches, washed, trimmed, chopped)
5 cups of chicken broth
1/4 cup of olive oil
2 tablespoons of garlic (minced)
1 tablespoon of red pepper flakes (crushed)
Salt and pepper

How to Make It:

Pour the 1/4 cup of olive oil in a large pot and turn to medium heat. Saute the 2 tablespoons of minced garlic. Pour in the 5 cups of chicken broth and add the smoked turkey drumstick. Cover and simmer for half an hour. Turn the heat up to medium high and add the 7 1/2 cups of collard greens. Keep the cover off, and stir occasionally, and cook for another 45 minutes. Turn the heat to medium, stir and add salt and pepper to taste and cook for another 50 minutes. Drain the liquid (keeping it for leftovers). Remove the meat (if necessary) from the turkey leg, discard the bone, shred and replace the meat and sprinkle and toss the tablespoon of crushed red pepper flakes.

Zucchini Fries

This is a delicious alternative to French fries, to enjoy a meal with fries while maintaining the metabolism diet. Makes 6 servings.

What You'll Need:

2 zucchinis (cut into three in "French fry" sized strips)
2 eggs
1/2 cup of almonds (ground)
1/2 cup of Parmesan cheese (grated)
1 tablespoon of salt
1/2 teaspoon of Italian herbs (dried)
Salt and pepper

How to Make It:

Prep: Preheat the oven to 425 degrees Fahrenheit. Spray a baking sheet with cooking spray or use a parchment liner.

After cutting the zucchinis place in a strainer and wash, then toss to get rid of excess water. Sprinkle the tablespoon of salt, and toss, while in the colander, and set aside for 60 minutes to air dry.

Crack the 2 eggs in a bowl and beat with a whisk. In a separate bowl, combine the 1/2 cup of ground almonds, 1/2 cup of grated Parmesan cheese, and the 1/2 teaspoon of dried Italian herbs. Dip each of the zucchini fries in the egg, then roll it through the nut mixture until all "fries" are coated. Lay out on the prepared baking sheet. Bake for 13 minutes in the hot oven, turn the fries over and bake for another 13 minutes, or until they reach a crisp golden brown. Salt and pepper to taste.

Seasoned Brussels Sprouts

This is a tasty and healthy side dish. People end up loving it after that first bite. Makes 8 servings.

What You'll Need:

2 pounds of Brussels sprouts (cored, shredded)
1/2 pound of turkey bacon
3 scallions (minced)
2/3 cup of pine nuts
1/4 cup of butter
1 tablespoon of canola oil
1/2 teaspoon of seasoning salt
Pepper

How to Make It:

Heat the tablespoon of canola oil in a skillet on medium high heat. "Fry" the half pound of turkey bacon. Crumble the bacon, reserve for later use. Add 1/4 cup of butter to the skillet and mix in with the canola oil. Stir in the 2/3 cup of pine nuts, and sauté. Stir in the 2 pounds of cored, shredded Brussels sprouts and the 3 minced scallions. Stir and sprinkle with the 1/2 teaspoon of seasoning salt and dashes of pepper to taste. Cook for 15 minutes. Toss in the crumbled turkey bacon and serve.

Seasoned Quinoa

Quinoa is a superfood and so incredibly nutritious. It takes the place of rice and pasta making an excellent side dish while maintaining the diet. Makes 4 servings.

What You'll Need:

2 cups of vegetable stock
1 cup of quinoa (uncooked)
1/2 cup of onions (chopped fine)
2 tablespoons of parsley (fresh chopped)
1 tablespoon of butter
1/2 tablespoon of thyme (fresh chopped)
2 teaspoons of garlic (minced)
Dash of lemon juice

How to Make It:

Place a saucepan on medium heat and add the tablespoon of butter. Once the butter melts, add the quinoa and stir for 5 minutes until nice and brown. Add the 2 cups of vegetable stock and turn the heat to high to bring to a boil. Turn to low, cover and simmer until the quinoa is tender enough to eat, about 15 minutes. Transfer the cooked quinoa to a serving bowl and toss in the 1/2 cup of onions (chopped fine), 2 tablespoons of parsley (fresh chopped), 1/2 tablespoon of thyme (fresh chopped), 2 teaspoons of garlic (minced), and a dash of lemon juice.

Cheesy Spinach Casserole

Get your green leafy vegetables in this super easy to cook delicious savory dish, made with cheese and spinach. Makes 6 servings.

What You'll Need:

20 oz. of spinach (2 -10 oz. frozen packages, chopped)
1 cup of cream cheese (softened)
1/4 cup of skim milk
1/3 cup of Parmesan cheese (grated)
Salt and pepper

How to Make It:

Prep: Preheat the oven to 350 degrees Fahrenheit.

Add the cup of softened cream cheese with the 1/4 cup of skim milk, stirring until combined. Add the 2 packages of frozen chopped spinach in a baking dish (1 quart). Spoon the cheese and milk mixture over the top of the spinach. Sprinkle salt and pepper to taste. Bake until hot, about 20 minutes.

Main Dish Recipes

Parmesan Chicken

This is a different Parmesan chicken, the "breading" is not breading at all but a batter made from mayonnaise, herbs and Parmesan cheese. Makes 6 servings.

What You'll Need:

3 chicken breasts (boneless, skinless, halved)
1 cup of mayonnaise
1/2 cup of Parmesan cheese (grated)
1 tablespoon of rosemary (fresh, chopped)
1 teaspoon of garlic (minced)
1 teaspoon of salt
Black pepper to taste

How to Make It:

Prep: Preheat oven to 350 degrees Fahrenheit. Line a 9x13 inch pan with foil.

In a bowl, combine the cup of mayonnaise with the tablespoon of fresh chopped rosemary, teaspoon of minced garlic, teaspoon of salt and a couple of dashes of black pepper (to taste). Place the 3 boneless, skinless, halved chicken breasts in the pan. Pour the mayonnaise mixture over the top, completely covering the chicken. Sprinkle the 1/2 cup of grated Parmesan cheese over the top. Bake until the chicken is well done (meat thermometer will read 160 degrees Fahrenheit in the thickest part, about 70 minutes.

Parmesan Tilapia

This is a delicious way to eat your fish, which is extremely healthy for your body and it tastes great to boot. Makes 8 servings.

What You'll Need:

2 pounds of tilapia fillets
1/2 cup of Parmesan cheese (grated)
1/4 cup of butter (soft)
3 tablespoons of mayonnaise
2 tablespoons of lemon juice
1/4 teaspoon of basil (dried)
1/4 teaspoon of black pepper (ground)
1/8 teaspoon of onion (powder)
1/8 teaspoon of celery salt

How to Make It:

Prep: Preheat the broiler on low. Line a baking sheet with foil and lightly spray with cooking spray.

Combine the 1/2 cup of grated Parmesan cheese, 1/4 cup of softened butter, with the 3 tablespoons of mayonnaise. Stir in the 2 tablespoons of lemon juice. Add the 1/4 teaspoon of basil (dried), 1/4 teaspoon of black pepper (ground), 1/8 teaspoon of onion (powder), and 1/8 teaspoon of celery salt and mix well. Set aside while the fish cooks. Meanwhile, place the 2 pound of tilapia fillets on the prepared baking sheet and broil on the top rack for 3 minutes on each side. Next, remove from the broiler and spread the Parmesan cheese mixture over all the fish, until coated. Place back under the hot broiler for another 2 to 3 minutes, fish is cooked when the coating turns a golden brown.

Grilled Shrimp

Shrimp is so quick and easy to fix, the toughest part of this recipe is creating the delicious marinade, and it is really not that tough. Makes 6 servings.

What You'll Need:

2 pounds of shrimp (fresh, deveined, peeled)
1/3 cup of olive oil
1/4 cup of tomato sauce
2 tablespoons of apple cider vinegar
2 tablespoons of basil (fresh chopped)
1 1/2 teaspoons of garlic (minced)
1/2 teaspoon of salt
1/4 teaspoon of cayenne pepper

How to Make It:

Mix the 1/3 cup of olive oil with the 1/4 cup of tomato sauce, and the 2 tablespoons of apple cider vinegar with a whisk. Stir in the 2 tablespoons of fresh chopped basil, 1 1/2 teaspoons of minced garlic, 1/2 teaspoon of salt, and the 1/4 teaspoon of cayenne pepper. Add the shrimp and toss to coat. Set in the refrigerator for an hour stir every 20 minutes. Preheat the grill on medium. Place the shrimp on skewers and grill for 3 minutes on each side.

Roasted Turkey

This is a delicious roasted turkey with savory herbs, enough to feed a small crowd.

What You'll Need:

1 turkey (at least 12 pounds)
4 cups of chicken stock
6 tablespoons of butter (divided into 6 pats)
2 tablespoons of parsley (dried)
2 tablespoons of onion (dried minced)
2 tablespoons of seasoning salt

How to Make It:

Prep: Preheat the oven to 350 degrees Fahrenheit. Rinse the turkey in cold water. Pull out the giblets and gravy packet (if available).

Set the washed turkey in a roasting pan. Pull the skin up and place the 6 pats of butter around under the skin. In a bowl, combine the 4 cups of chicken stock, 2 tablespoons of parsley (dried), and the 2 tablespoons of onion (dried minced). Pour the seasoned chicken stock over the turkey then spread the 2 tablespoons of seasoning salt over the top. Cover the bird tightly with foil and bake for 3 hours and 15 minutes. Remove the foil and bake until a meat thermometer inserted into the meaty part reads 180 degrees Fahrenheit, about 45 more minutes. If desired and if available, you may fix the gravy packet.

Roasted Chicken

Another delicious meat dish cooked with savory seasonings and celery. Makes 6 servings.

What You'll Need:

1 chicken (at least 3 pounds, whole)
1/2 cup of butter (in pieces)
1/2 cup of celery (quartered)
1 tablespoon of onion (powder)
salt and pepper

How to Make It:

Prep: Preheat the oven to 350 degrees Fahrenheit.

Rinse the chicken and pat dry remove the giblets. Place on a roasting pan, legs up, sprinkling it all over with the salt and pepper. Next sprinkle it all over with the onion powder, using at least 1 tablespoon or more if desired. Add the chopped 1/2 cup of butter all over the chicken, inside the cavity and around on the top. Place the 1/2 cup of quartered celery in the chicken cavity. Bake until the meat reaches 180 degrees Fahrenheit, about 75 minutes. Remove from oven, turn oven off and with a spoon or turkey baster, and baste the chicken with the drippings. Tightly cover the chicken with foil and replace back in the warmed oven to sit for half an hour before serving.

Home Style Rotisserie Chicken

If you love the deli rotisserie chicken, you can make this recipe at home now. Makes around 8 servings.

What You'll Need:

2 chickens (whole, 4 pounds each)
1 cup of onions (quartered)
4 teaspoons of salt
2 teaspoons of paprika
1 teaspoon of onion (powder)
1 teaspoon of white pepper
1 teaspoon of thyme (dried)
1/2 teaspoon of black pepper
1/2 teaspoon of cayenne pepper
1/2 teaspoon of garlic powder

How to Make It:

Rinse the chicken in water and pat dry, removing any giblets. Combine the 4 teaspoons of salt, 2 teaspoons of paprika, 1 teaspoon of onion (powder), 1 teaspoon of white pepper, 1 teaspoon of thyme (dried), 1/2 teaspoon of black pepper, 1/2 teaspoon of cayenne pepper, and the 1/2 teaspoon of garlic powder. Rub the seasonings all over the outside and inside of the chicken.

Divide the quartered cup of onions and place inside each chicken cavity. Tightly wrap the chickens in plastic wrap. Refrigerate for either 6 hours or overnight. After refrigeration, preheat the oven to 250 degrees Fahrenheit. Remove the chickens from the plastic wrap and place on a roasting pan, legs up. Bake until meat temperature reaches 180 degrees Fahrenheit with a meat thermometer, about 5 hours. Allow to cool out of the oven for 10 minutes before serving.

Baked Shrimp Scampi

A delicious main dish of shrimp with a hint of Dijon mustard.

What You'll Need:

2 pounds of shrimp (peeled, deveined, leave tails)
1/2 cup of butter
1 tablespoons of Dijon mustard
1 tablespoon of lemon juice
1 tablespoon of garlic (chopped)
1 tablespoons of parsley (fresh chopped)

How to Make It:

Prep: Preheat oven to 450 degrees Fahrenheit.

Heat a saucepan on medium and add the 1/2 cup of butter, 1 tablespoons of Dijon mustard, 1 tablespoon of lemon juice, 1 tablespoon of garlic (chopped), and 1 tablespoons of parsley (fresh chopped), stir until the butter melts, then remove from the stove. Add the shrimp to the bottom of a baking dish, pour the melted butter and spices over the shrimp. Place in the oven and bake for around 13 minutes, removing when the shrimp turns pink. Serve immediately.

Spicy Marinated Grilled Shrimp

This shrimp tastes delicious hot of the skewer right from the grill, be careful it has a spicy bite!

What You'll Need:

2 pounds of shrimp (peeled, deveined, tails intact)
1 cup of olive oil
1/4 cup of parsley (fresh chopped)
2 tablespoons of lemon juice
2 tablespoons of hot pepper sauce
1 tablespoon of tomato paste
2 teaspoons of oregano (dried)
1 1/2 teaspoons of garlic (minced)
1 teaspoon of salt
1 teaspoon of black pepper (ground)

How to Make It:

Combine the 1 cup of olive oil, 1/4 cup of parsley (fresh chopped), 2 tablespoons of lemon juice, 2 tablespoons of hot pepper sauce, 1 tablespoon of tomato paste, 2 teaspoons of oregano (dried), 1 1/2 teaspoons of garlic (minced), 1 teaspoon of salt, and 1 teaspoon of black pepper (ground) in a bowl with a whisk. Pull off about 2 tablespoons and set aside for later. Add the 2 pounds of peeled, deveined, tailed shrimp into a large zipper seal bag, and pour the marinade over. Zip the bag shut and make sure all shrimp are well coated. Place the bag in a large bowl to prevent leaks and set in the refrigerator for at least 2 hours. Heat the grill to medium low, skewer the shrimp and grill for at least 5 minutes on each side. Baste with the reserved marinade during the cooking. Serve immediately.

Marinated Grilled Turkey Breast

A delicious main dish made with a tasty marinade and healthy turkey breast. There is one tablespoon of brown sugar in the marinade, but since it is spread out over 6 pounds of turkey, very little of it is actually ingested.

What You'll Need:

2 turkey breast halves (3 pounds each)
1/4 cup of canola oil
1/4 cup of soy sauce
2 tablespoons of lemon juice
1 tablespoon of basil (fresh, fine chopped)
1 tablespoon of brown sugar
6 cloves (whole)
1 teaspoon of garlic (minced)
1/2 teaspoon of pepper

How to Make It:

Rinse the turkey breasts with cold water and pat dry. Make a rub out of the tablespoon of fresh fine chopped basil, teaspoon of minced garlic, and the 1/2 teaspoon of pepper. Rub the seasonings all over the 2 3 pound turkey breasts. Add two cloves inside each turkey breasts and sprinkle the rest between the two. Make the marinade by adding 1/4 cup of canola oil, 1/4 cup of soy sauce, 2 tablespoons of lemon juice, and tablespoon of brown sugar, combined with a whisk and pour into a shallow dish. Add the turkey breasts, rolling to coat all sides, cover tightly with a lid, plastic wrap, or foil. Refrigerate for 4 or more hours. Grill on high heat until a meat thermometer inserted in the middle of a breast ready 170 degrees Fahrenheit, should take about half an hour, turning the breasts half way through.

Italian Meatballs

These are delicious spooned onto a plate and served with vegetables. Makes 8 servings.

What You'll Need:

2 pounds of ground beef (lean)
2 cups of "stale" Flat Bread with Flax crumbs (recipe in this book)
1 1/4 cups of water (lukewarm)
1 cup of olive oil
1 cup of Romano cheese (fine grated)
2 eggs
1 1/2 tablespoons of Parsley (Italian flat leaf)
1 teaspoon of garlic (minced)
Salt and pepper

How to Make It:

Add the 2 pounds of lean ground beef to a large bowl. Crack the 2 eggs and beat in a cup, then pour into the meat along with the 1 cup of fine grated Romano cheese, 1 1/2 tablespoons of Italian flat leaf parsley, teaspoon of minced garlic and dashes of salt and pepper. Mix with clean hands. Add the 2 cups of stale Flat Bread with Flax crumbs, working it in evenly throughout the meat. Add the 1 1/4 cups of lukewarm water very slow adding a bit mixing, add more, and repeat. Shape into meatballs (however big you wish to make them.) Heat the cup of olive oil in a large frying pan. Add a few meatballs, leaving enough room to roll them to brown on all sides. Meatballs are done when the outside turns slightly crisp. Repeat until all are cooked, serve, and enjoy.

Herbed Steaks

These tasty steaks makes for a great main course coupled with steamed vegetables or a salad. The tiny bit of sugar helps to marinade the steaks and it is so little it does not amount to much per serving. Makes 6 servings.

What You'll Need:

2 pounds of beef steaks (trimmed chuck)
1/3 cup of apple cider vinegar
1/3 cup of water
1 tablespoon of olive oil
1 tablespoon of thyme (fresh chopped)
1/2 teaspoon of sugar (granulated)

How to Make It:

Mix the 1/3 cup of apple cider vinegar, 1/3 cup of water, 1 tablespoon of olive oil, 1 tablespoon of thyme (fresh chopped), and the 1/2 teaspoon of sugar (granulated) using a whisk. Place the steaks in a dish and pour the marinade on top, making sure all meat is covered. Let it sit in the refrigerator overnight or for 8 hours. Heat the grill to medium and cook each steak on the oiled rack for up to 26 minutes, to the desired done-ness.

Italian Cod

Remember, fish is nutritious full of goodness, excellent nutrients for the brain. Have it a couple of times a week. Makes 4 servings.

What You'll Need:

4 cod fillets (at least 3 oz. each)
1 egg white (slightly beaten)
1/4 cup of dry bread crumbs (use the Flat Bread with Flax recipe)
2 tablespoons of Parmesan cheese (grated)
1 tablespoon of cornmeal
1 teaspoon of olive oil
1/2 teaspoon of Italian seasoning
1/8 teaspoon of garlic (powder)
1/8 teaspoon of pepper

How to Make It:

Prep: Preheat the oven to 450 degrees Fahrenheit. Spray the rack of the broiler pan with cooking spray.

Combine the 1/4 cup of dry bread crumbs (use the Flat Bread with Flax recipe), 2 tablespoons of Parmesan cheese (grated), 1 tablespoon of cornmeal, 1 teaspoon of olive oil, 1/2 teaspoon of Italian seasoning, 1/8 teaspoon of garlic (powder), and 1/8 teaspoon of pepper in a small bowl. Place the 4 cod fillets on the boiler pan rack. Brush the slightly beaten egg whites over the tops of the cod, and then sprinkle the crumb coating over the top. Bake for 11 minutes, when the coating is a golden brown and crispy.

Seafood Stew

There is nothing more filling than a bowl of seafood stew, enough to stick to the ribs (but not the waistline!) and keep the hunger away. Makes 8 servings.

What You'll Need:

1 pound of shrimp (peeled, deveined)
1 pound of bay scallops
1 pound of cod fillets (cubed)
10 clams (small)
10 mussels (debearded, cleaned)
1 can of stewed tomatoes (14.5 oz.)
1 1/2 cups of chicken stock
1 cup of white grape juice
2/3 cup of crabmeat
3/4 cup of parsley (fresh chopped)
3/4 cup of onions (chopped)
1/2 cup of water
1/3 cup of butter
1 bay leaf
1 3/4 teaspoons of basil (dried)
3/4 teaspoon of garlic (minced)
1/4 teaspoon of thyme (dried)
1/4 teaspoon of oregano (dried)

How to Make It:

Place a large stockpot over medium low heat and add the 1/3 cup of butter to melt. Stir in the 3/4 cup of fresh chopped parsley, 3/4 cup of chopped onions, and 3/4 teaspoon of minced garlic and sauté. Add the 1 can of stewed tomatoes (14.5 oz.), 1 1/2 cups of chicken stock, 1 cup of white grape juice, 3/4 cup of parsley (fresh chopped), 1/2 cup of water, 1 bay leaf, 1 3/4 teaspoons of basil (dried), 3/4 teaspoon of garlic (minced), 1/4 teaspoon of thyme (dried), and
1/4 teaspoon of oregano (dried) and stir. Cover the pot and turn heat to low to simmer for half an hour. Add the 1 pound of shrimp (peeled, deveined),1 pound of bay scallops, 1 pound of cod fillets (cubed), 10 clams (small), 10 mussels (debearded, cleaned), and the 2/3 cup of crabmeat and turn heat to high to bring to a boil, then reduce heat to low, replace the lid and cook for an additional 7 minutes. Remove and discard the bay leaf.

Egg Salad

This makes for a light supper or even a good lunch, the egg salad is a perfect spread for one of the bread recipes within this book. Makes 4 servings.

What You'll Need:

8 eggs
1/4 cup of onion (minced)
2 tablespoons of mayonnaise
1 tablespoon of yellow mustard
1 teaspoon of dill weed
1 teaspoon of paprika
Salt and pepper

How to Make It:

Put the 8 eggs in a saucepan, cover to about half an inch over the top of the eggs with cold water. Place saucepan on high heat and bring water to a boil. Boil for 10 minutes; turn off heat, let stand for 5 minutes. Place saucepan under the faucet and run cold water to cool the eggs. Peel the eggshells, cut the eggs in half, remove the egg yolks to a small bowl, and mince the egg whites and place in a small serving bowl. In the egg yolk bowl, combine with the 2 tablespoons of mayonnaise, tablespoon of yellow mustard until smooth. Next stir in the teaspoon of dill weed, teaspoon of paprika, and salt and pepper. Finally, toss the1/4 cup of minced onions with the egg whites and pour the dressing over, tossing, and mixing well. Let it sit in the refrigerator for half an hour at least before serving.

Slow Cooked Italian Beef

This is a delicious and savory beef, so tender it falls off the fork. It is perfect with a meal of fresh vegetables, a salad, or on a sandwich. Makes 10 servings.

What You'll Need:

1 rump roast (beef, 5 lbs.)
1 package of Italian-style dressing mix (dry)
2 cups of water
1 cup of beef stock
1 bay leaf
1 teaspoon of basil (dried)
1 teaspoon of garlic (powdered)
1 teaspoon of onion salt
1 teaspoon of oregano (dried)
1 teaspoon of parsley (dried)
1 teaspoon of pepper
1 teaspoon of salt

How to Make It:

Pour the 2 cups of water and the cup of beef stock into a saucepan along with the 1 cup of beef stock, 1 bay leaf, 1 teaspoon of basil (dried), 1 teaspoon of garlic (powdered), 1 teaspoon of onion salt, 1 teaspoon of oregano (dried), 1 teaspoon of parsley (dried), 1 teaspoon of pepper, and 1 teaspoon of salt and bring the liquid to a boil while stirring over high heat. Put the 5 lb. beef rump roast in a large slow cooker and pour the hot liquid over the roast. Cover and cook on high for 5 hours, or low for 10 hours. Remove and discard the bay leaf, shred the beef, and serve.

Garlic Parmesan Chicken

This recipe makes a delicious main dish chicken, serve with steamed vegetables and a salad. Makes 4 servings.

What You'll Need:

4 chicken breast halves (boneless, skinless)
1/4 cup of olive oil
1/4 cup of dry bread crumbs (from the Flat Bread with Flax recipe)
1/4 cup of Parmesan cheese (grated)
2 teaspoons of garlic (minced)

How to Make It:

Prep: Preheat the oven to 425 degrees Fahrenheit. Line a shallow baking dish with foil.

Pour the 1/4 cup of olive oil into a saucepan on medium heat. Add the 2 teaspoons of minced garlic and heat until very warm. In a shallow dish, add the 1/4 cup of dry bread crumbs with the 1/4 cup of grated Parmesan cheese, mixing well. Next, dip each chicken breast half into the warmed olive oil and garlic, then roll in the bread crumb and Parmesan cheese mixture. Place the "breaded" chicken breasts onto the lined baking dish.

Bake until the chicken is done, about 35 minutes.

Meatloaf

This is a delicious meatloaf recipe, one that is as good as leftovers as it is fresh. Makes 8 servings.

What You'll Need:

2 pounds of ground beef (lean)
1 cup of bread crumbs (made from the Flat Bread with Flax recipe)
1 egg
1/2 cup of ketchup (divided)
1/4 cup of water
1 tablespoon of onions (dried)
1 tablespoon of Greek seasoning

How to Make It:

Preheat the oven to 350 degrees Fahrenheit. Line a regular sized loaf pan with foil.

In a large bowl, break up the 2 pounds of lean ground beef with your hands. Mix in the cup of breadcrumbs. Crack an egg in a cup, beat, then add to the meat mixture along with 1/4 cup of ketchup, 1/4 cup of water, 1 tablespoon of onions (dried), and 1 tablespoon of Greek seasoning. Mix well, and then form into a loaf and place in the loaf pan. Pour the remaining ketchup over the top of the meat. Place in the hot oven and bake for about an hour or until a meat thermometer reaches 160 degrees Fahrenheit. Let cool for 5 to 10 minutes before serving.

Section 2: Intermittent Fasting Diet

What is the intermittent fasting diet?

This is a diet in which you eat during specified time frames. There are two popular versions of this diet. One being a day to day eat and fast where you eat on day one, fast on day two, and repeat until the desired weight is lost. The other version is a daily fasting, where you eat for a six to eight hour and then fast the rest of the day.

Starting out on the intermittent fasting diet

Please be aware that results from the intermittent diet vary from person to person. Much of the variance depends upon the build of the body, how much fat, and weight need to be lost and how they eat during the diet. Other factors that influence weight loss are lifestyle (do you smoke? drink? eat excessive junk food?), insulin resistance, exercise or not, and work. All these things work towards either making it difficult to lose the weight or to lose it fast. No two people are alike, even if they each desire to lose the same amount of weight. Keeping this in mind helps you to tailor the diet to your own needs.

Intermittent means eating and fasting in chunks of time. You may need to adjust this as you go along, to help deal with other health issues, to speed things along or to help improve health. Be ready to make adjustments and learn how to bend with the changes. Keeping a positive attitude will carry you a long ways in having good success in this diet.

This is a great diet to start for good weight loss. When the weight and fat are gone you can go on a maintenance, where you may still continue to fast, but more on a less restriction.

Other Issues Helped By Intermittent Fasting

If you suffer from any type of insulin or blood sugar problems, the metabolism is improved by fasting, eating in this manner. Eating through a fasting manner helps the body to lower inflammation rates, helps to improve blood pressure, helps to release stress, and helps to boost the immune system. If the immune system is boosted, the body is able to fight off other illnesses and keep you healthy and strong. Because this diet helps also to increase metabolism (especially if you eat the right food) you will have more energy to exercise and your body will have more energy to digest and disperse the foods you eat.

One of the biggest reasons people gain so much weight is they feel the need to eat all the time. This constant eating causes people to grab for the fast, convenient, and high in sugar and salt foods. These foods are responsible for putting a massive amount of weight on those who gorge. The intermittent fasting diet stops this binge eating and helps to creating a habit of eating during the best times of the day.

The Basics of the Intermittent Fasting Diet

The intermittent fasting diet is an extremely flexible diet plan. There are no set rules for doing it other than having a nice solid block of time to fast. As mentioned above one of the methods of fasting involves taking a day or longer of no food, and doing this a couple of times a week. For obvious reasons, this mode is a lot tougher to deal with, as going a solid day without food may be impossible for some people, especially for those with blood sugar issues.

Daily intermittent fasting is better because it does allow for the intake of food on a daily basis. But it also means for a strict window of daily fasting too and this is what helps to facilitate the weight loss. Basically you eat during a six to eight hour time and fast the remainder.

Your lifestyle will directly affect the effectiveness of this diet. Because the diet is flexible, there are no set foods or meals to eat during the six to eight hour window, just to eat. If you are in the habit of consuming a lot of carbohydrates, (sugars, white flours, and basically food with no nutritious value) then your weight loss may not happen or may be very slow. If your lifestyle is very sedentary, it will take longer to lose the weight.

Here is the thing, if you clean up your eating habits and eat foods packed with nutrition, it will give your body the energy to burn to move about more. You will want to exercise and move about more. Your digestive system will also work more efficiently, digesting in a time and manner that will get rid of the fat and calories.

Choosing the Daily Intermittent Fasting

This book is geared to offer recipes for the daily plan. It is easier to follow the daily fasting routine and can be developed into a habit, which will help it to be easier to do. You will break bad habits of needing to binge or gorge on food, because you know that after your six to eight hours, you simply will not eat. Your body will be able to adjust to this much easier, because you will have food in your body daily. If you eat the right foods, your body will have nutrients in which to work to help keep you healthier.

Snacking is the downfall of many who may eat well during the meals but find themselves reaching for foods void of nutrients. Unfortunately, these types of foods are highly addictive, the more we consume them the more our bodies want it. But it is also a habit that is fairly easy to break if you have the will power to do so. This diet stops the constant snacking.

By fasting on a daily basis, you will be more aware of your body. The hope is you will be aware of the foods you eat during the feeding hours, and will choose to consume healthier foods and snacks.

Be Aware Of Issues

If you do not consume enough calories during the feeding window, you can run the risk of reaching a weight loss plateau. This occurs when the body is too restricted from food (remember what we discussed about "starvation mode" above?) This can be avoided by eating the right foods. If you consume junk foods, then your body will not have substantial energy to keep going during the fasting period. If you eat a balance of good complex carbohydrates, proteins, and nutrients, your body can easily sustain the diet and the body during the fasting.

Some people will not be able to do the intermittent fasting diet. Some people have a greater need for more calories and they simply will not perform well unless they are consuming these calories. It is wise to have a physical and make sure your body can handle such a diet. Go over your choices with your health care provider and let them help you to decide whether or not this diet is right and healthy for you.

Making the Intermittent Diet a Success

This diet can be a great success if you do it right. It does take work and dedication though. First thing is to eat right. Choose foods that are healthy and whole during your feeding and avoid junk foods altogether. Eat a good breakfast each morning that will fuel your body to keep it going during the day. Choose healthy snacks. In the sample 5 day meal plan we suggest to eat fruit and nuts to snack. It is okay to drink fruit juice and eat leftovers or a small meal if you would rather. The point is to consume foods like lean meats, fruits, vegetables, and whole grains that help to give the body all the nutrients it needs to function at optimum levels.

Once the feeding window closes, do not consume any more food until the next day. It is okay and encouraged, though, to drink plenty of water throughout the entire day. Water helps to facilitate weight loss and helps to cleanse the body of impurities and toxins. Try drinking water throughout the feeding window as well. It helps with digestion too.

Take up an exercise routine. If your body is moving around it helps to burn more calories. Exercise also helps the body to release endorphins, and these are nature's way of giving you a natural high. Exercise is addictive too, the more you do it the more you will want to do it. The toughest part is starting. Even if you only work out three times a week for thirty minutes each time, you are giving your body a greater chance of fat and weight loss by doing so.

Sample 5 Day Meal Plan

The three meals here are smaller portions than a regular meal. The meals are to be eaten in a 6 to 8 hour time frame, with a 16 to 18 time frame of fasting. During the fasting time, you can have water. It is okay to have more with the meals if you are hungry. Try having a salad with lunch and supper if needed. Drink plenty of water during the day too.

Day One

Breakfast - Tomato Spinach Eggs
Snack - Nuts
Lunch - Edamame and Grilled Salmon
Snack - Fruit
Supper - Apple and Turkey Ham Salad

Day Two

Breakfast - Whole Grain Hot Cereal with Cherries
Snack - Nuts
Lunch - Balsamic Turkey Meatloaf
Snack - Fruit
Supper - Broccoli Cheese Soup

Day Three

Breakfast - Savory Hash Browns
Snack - Nuts
Lunch Buffalo Chicken with Slaw
Snack - Fruit
Supper - Open Face Tomato and Mozzarella Herb

Sandwich

Day Four

Breakfast - Mexican Breakfast Casserole
Snack - Nuts
Lunch - Shrimp Scampi
Snack - Fruit
Supper - Spinach Salad with Pomegranate Dressing

Day Five

Breakfast - Healthy Breakfast Burrito
Snack - Nuts
Lunch - Italian Chicken
Snack - Fruit
Supper - Baked Potatoes Twice

Intermittent Fasting Diet Recipes

Intermittent Fasting Diet Breakfast Recipes

Breakfast Casserole

This makes a perfect brunch because it is a hearty and filling casserole of eggs, cheese, tomatoes, and English muffins. This recipe needs to be prepared the night before. Makes 8 servings.

What You'll Need:

4 English muffins (halved, toasted)
4 scallions (cut into long bite-sized pieces)
4 eggs plus 3 egg whites
3 cups of milk (low fat)
2/3 cup of cheddar cheese (extra sharp, shredded, divided)
3/4 cup of deli ham (torn, thin slices)
1/2 cup of tomatoes (no oil, sundried, sliced)
1 tablespoon of Dijon mustard

Salt and pepper

How to Make It:

Spray a 2-quart baking dish with cooking spray. Layer the bottom of the pan with the 4 halved and toasted English muffins and the 3/4 cup of torn thin sliced deli ham, making sure to lay it out evenly. Next layer it with the 4 scallions cut into bite-sized pieces, 1/2 cup of sliced sundried tomatoes, and 1/3 cup of shredded extra sharp cheddar cheese. In a bowl, crack the 4 eggs and add the 3 egg whites and beat with a whisk, then combine with the 3 cups of low fat milk, tablespoon of Dijon mustard and dashes of salt and pepper. Pour the egg mixture over the layered casserole in the baking dish. Add the remaining 1/3 cup of extra sharp cheddar cheese on top. Cover tightly with plastic wrap and refrigerate overnight. Next morning, preheat the oven to 350 degrees Fahrenheit. Remove the plastic wrap and cook the casserole (with a baking sheet under it) for 60 minutes. Remove from oven and let it sit for at least 10 minutes to set and cool before serving and enjoying.

Healthy Breakfast Burrito

Mornings are the time to refuel for the day. Start the day right with a breakfast burrito that is as healthy as it is delicious. Makes 4 servings.

What You'll Need:

4 tortillas (whole wheat, burrito)
4 eggs
4 egg whites
1 avocado (cubed)
1 cup of onions (diced)
1 cup of black beans (cooked, rinsed)
3/4 cup of tomatoes (diced)
1/2 cup of bell peppers (red, seeded, diced)
1/3 cup of pepper Jack cheese (shredded)
1/4 cup of sour cream
1/4 cup of salsa
2 teaspoons of canola oil
1/4 teaspoon of red pepper flakes
Salt and pepper
Hot sauce

How to Make It:

Add the 2 teaspoons of canola oil to a skillet on medium

high heat. Sauté the 1/2 cup of seeded, diced red bell peppers and 1/2 cup of diced onions. Stir in the cup of cooked, rinsed black beans and the 1/4 teaspoon of red pepper flakes. Cook for a couple of minutes to warm, and then add dashes of salt and pepper. Put the contents into a bowl and set aside. In a separate bowl crack the 4 eggs and add the additional 4 egg whites and whisk. Add the 1/3 cup of shredded pepper Jack cheese. Spray the same skillet with cooking spray, heat to medium and scramble the eggs until done. In a separate non-stick skillet, heat to medium, and warm each tortilla on each side for about 30 seconds. Next, to build the burrito, add 1/4 of the sour cream and 1/4 of the salsa followed by 1/4 of the black beans and topped with 1/4 of the eggs and then season with extra salt, pepper, and hot sauce. Roll up and serve. Do this with each one.

Mexican Style Eggs "Huevos Rancheros"

If you love Mexican food, you will love your breakfast fixed fiesta style. Makes 4 servings.

What You'll Need:

4 eggs
4 tortillas (corn, 6 inch, warmed)
1 can of black beans (15.5 oz, drained, rinsed)
1 jalapeno pepper (minced)
1 1/2 cups of tomatoes (fine chopped)
1/2 cup of onions (fine chopped)
1/2 cup of feta cheese (crumbled)
1/2 cup of water (warm)
1/4 cup of cilantro (fresh chopped)
2 tablespoons of olive oil (plus 2 teaspoons, extra virgin)
1 teaspoon of garlic (minced)
1 teaspoon of cumin (ground)
1/2 teaspoon of hot sauce
Salt and pepper

How to Make It:

Mix the 1 jalapeno pepper (minced), 1 1/2 cups of tomatoes (fine chopped), 1/2 cup of onions (fine chopped), 1 teaspoon of garlic (minced), 1 teaspoon of cumin (ground), 1/2 teaspoon of hot sauce, and dashes of salt and pepper together to make salsa. Pour 2 teaspoons of olive oil into a skillet and heat to medium low. Pour in the "salsa" mixture and stir for a couple of minutes until it thickens. Pour the salsa in a bowl and set to the side. Add the can of drained, rinsed black beans along with 1/2 cup of warm water and another dash of salt into the skillet. Cover, turn heat to low and simmer while preparing the rest of the eggs. Add the 2 tablespoons of extra virgin olive oil to another skillet and heat to medium. Crack the eggs, one at a time to make 4 fried eggs, or sunny side up. Season with salt and pepper. Warm the 4 tortillas by placing on a plate with a damp paper towel on top and microwave for about 20 seconds. Next, place a tortilla on 4 plates. Equally divide the beans on top of the 4 tortillas. Add a fried egg to each one. Add a spoon of salsa on top of each egg, and then divide the 1/2 cup of feta cheese crumbles on top of the salsa. Garnish with the 1/4 cup of fresh chopped cilantro and the rest of the salsa. Serve immediately.

Mexican Breakfast Casserole

Here is a casserole filled with the spiciness of chili and cilantro, delicious and filling. Makes 6 servings.

What You'll Need:

4 cups of tortilla chips (baked, divided)
4 eggs plus 6 extra egg whites
1 can of green chilies (chopped, drained)
1/2 cup of cheddar cheese (sharp, shredded - divided)
1/2 cup of pepper Jack cheese (shredded - divided)
1/2 cup of salsa (green Verde)
1/4 cup of skim milk
1 tablespoon of cilantro (fresh chopped plus more for garnishment)
3/4 teaspoon of ancho chili powder
Dollops of sour cream
Salt and pepper

How to Make It:

Prep: Preheat the oven to 375 degrees Fahrenheit. Spray a 2 quart baking dish with cooking spray.

Crumble the 4 cups of baked tortilla chips (large crumbles) and lay 2 cups of chips in the bottom of the baking dish. In a bowl, crack the 4 eggs and add the 6 egg whites and beat with a whisk. Add the 1/4 cup of skim milk, 3/4 teaspoon of ancho chili powder, and dashes of salt and pepper and stir. Mix in the can of chopped drained green chilies, 1/4 cup of shredded sharp cheddar cheese, 1/4 cup of shredded pepper Jack cheese, and the tablespoon of fresh chopped cilantro. Pour the mixture over the baked tortilla chips in the baking dish. Place in hot oven and bake for about 22 minutes, until the eggs are set. Pull out of oven and sprinkle the remaining 1/4 cup of shredded sharp cheddar cheese and the 1/4 cup of shredded pepper Jack cheese and place back in the oven for 10 more minutes. Pull from oven, turn heat off, and allow sitting for another 10 minutes. Serve with a spoon of green Verde salsa, dollop of sour cream, and a garnishment of cilantro leaf.

Savory Hash Browns

All you need to do is cook up and egg and have a piece of whole grain toast and you are set for a meal. Makes 4 servings.

What You'll Need:

2 potatoes (Yukon gold, washed, grated - with skins)
2 scallions (chopped)
1 parsnip (peeled, grated)
2 tablespoons of parsley (minced flat leaf)
1 tablespoon of olive oil (extra virgin, divided)
Salt and pepper

How to Make It:

Toss the 2 grated potatoes with the grated parsnip, add the 2 chopped scallions, greens and all. Season with dashes of salt and pepper. Pour the 1/2 tablespoon of extra virgin olive oil into a skillet and heat to medium. Stir in the grated potatoes, parsnips, and scallions, tossing to coat with oil, then press down into the skillet, once in a while, run the spatula under the mixture to prevent sticking. Cook until crispy brown for around 10 minutes. Flip the mixture out onto a large dinner plate. Add the remaining 1/2 tablespoon of olive oil, return skillet to heat, then replace the mixture, uncooked side down to crisp the other side, another 10 minutes. Serve hot.

Squash, Zucchini and Eggs

This is a great summer meal using fresh squash if possible. Makes 6 servings.

What You'll Need:

6 eggs
4 scallions (sliced thin, greens separated out)
3 squash (grated)
3 zucchini (grated)
1 jalapeno (seeded, minced)
1/4 cup of cheddar cheese (sharp white, shredded)
1/4 cup of pepper jack (shredded)
3 tablespoons of parsley (fresh chopped)
2 tablespoons of olive oil (extra virgin)
1 tablespoon of butter
1 tablespoon of salt
1/4 teaspoon of nutmeg (ground)
Salt and pepper

How to Make It:

Toss the 3 shredded squash and the 3 grated zucchinis with a tablespoon of salt while they rest in a colander for 35 minutes. Using a paper towel, squeeze the squash and zucchini.

Preheat the oven to 375 degrees Fahrenheit. Place an oven proof (cast iron works well) skillet on the stove on medium high heat. Pour in the 2 tablespoons of extra virgin olive oil. Reserve 3 tablespoons of the greens from the 4 scallions and put the remainder of the greens and all the whites into the heated oil along with the seeded minced jalapeno and sauté. Toss in the grated squash and zucchini, stir, and toss for about 7 minutes. Add the 3 tablespoons of fresh chopped parsley, 1/4 teaspoon of ground nutmeg, and dashes of salt, pepper, and stir, cooking for another minute. Remove skillet from the stove and sit for 5 minutes away from the heat. Next, pat the squash, zucchini mixture down, then with the back of a serving spoon make 6 indentions, spaced evenly over the squash and zucchini. Place 1/2 of a teaspoon of butter into each of the 6 indentions. Carefully, crack an egg in a cup, then pour right into and indention, with all 6 eggs. Sprinkle dashes of salt and pepper over the eggs. Add the remaining 1/4 cups of shredded sharp cheddar cheese and pepper Jack cheese, evenly over the top. Carefully place the skillet in the hot oven and bake for about 11 minutes. Garnish with the 3 tablespoons of the chopped green scallions and serve immediately.

Tomato Spinach Eggs

This is a delicious way to get protein and vegetables first thing in the morning, with this savory eggs Benedict recipe. Makes 4 servings.

What You'll Need:

8 cups of spinach (fresh baby)
4 slices of tomato (large slices)
4 eggs
2 English Muffins (split in half)
1/2 cup of onions (thin sliced)
1/3 cup of Canadian bacon (chunked)
1/4 cup of vinegar (white distilled)
2 tablespoons of mayonnaise
1 tablespoon of water (warm)
1 tablespoon of olive oil
2 teaspoons of mustard
1 teaspoon of lemon juice
Dash of cayenne pepper
Pepper

How to Make It:

Make the sauce by combining the 2 tablespoons of mayonnaise, 1 tablespoon of water (warm), 2 teaspoons of mustard, 1 teaspoon of lemon juice, and dash of cayenne pepper with a whisk.

Next, start the Benedict eggs by adding several inches of water to a large saucepan. Pour in the 1/4 cup of white distilled vinegar and turn the heat to medium.

Set a nonstick frying pan on medium high, add the tablespoon of olive oil, 1/3 cup of Canadian bacon chunks, and the 1/2 cup of onions, and cook until heated through. Stir in the 8 cups of fresh baby spinach, take the frying pan off the heat, and continue stirring for a couple of minutes until the leaves wilt. Sprinkle pepper and toss.

Pop the English muffins into a toaster to toast lightly on all sides. Set them on a serving platter and top with a slice of tomato. Add 1/4 of the Canadian bacon mixture on top of each tomato slice.

Next, cook one egg at a time, buy cracking into a small dish, then pouring into the simmering vinegar water. Cook for about 4 minutes. Remove and place on top of the Canadian bacon on the English muffin halves. Do this with all 4 eggs. Spoon the hollandaise sauce over the top and serve hot.

Whole Grain Hot Cereal with Cherries

There is nothing heartier than a bowl of hot whole grain cereal first thing in the morning. You will enjoy this meal with the aroma and flavor of fruit making it a delightful meal. Makes 4 servings.

What You'll Need:

5 cups of water
1/2 cup of rice (wild)
1/2 cup of oats (steel-cut)
1/2 cup of wheat cereal (cream of wheat)
1/4 cup of pearl barley
1/4 cup of cherries (dried)
1 cinnamon stick
1 1/2 tablespoons of brown sugar (packed)
1/2 teaspoon of orange zest
1/4 teaspoon of salt
Walnuts (chopped)
Butter
Milk

How to Make It:

The evening before add the 5 cups of water, 1/2 cup of rice (wild), 1/2 cup of oats (steel-cut), 1/2 cup of wheat cereal (cream of wheat), 1/4 cup of pearl barley, 1/4 cup of cherries (dried), 1 cinnamon stick, 1 1/2 tablespoons of brown sugar (packed), 1/2 teaspoon of orange zest, and 1/4 teaspoon of salt and stir in a large sauce pan. Place the cover and let sit on the stove with the heat off over night. The morning of breakfast, turn the stove on high and bring to a boil, then turn it down on low to simmer, cover on for 20 minutes. Keep the cover on, turn the stove off and let it sit for another 5 minutes. Serve in bowls and garnish with chopped walnuts, butter and milk if desired.

Whole Wheat Pancakes with Apples

Pancakes are always fun to cook and eat. You cannot go wrong with this recipe, which uses whole-wheat flour to give you the benefit of whole grains, and the goodness of fresh apples. Makes 6 servings.

What You'll Need:

1 cup of buttermilk (low fat)
3/4 cup of skim milk
3/4 cup of apples (cored, diced)
3/4 cup of flour (all-purpose)
3/4 cup of flour (whole-wheat)
2 eggs
6 tablespoons of maple syrup
1 tablespoon of honey
2 teaspoons of baking powder
1/2 teaspoon of baking soda
1/4 teaspoon of salt

How to Make It:

Prep: Preheat the oven to 250 degrees Fahrenheit.

In a bowl, combine the 3/4 cup of flour (all-purpose), 3/4 cup of flour (whole-wheat), 2 teaspoons of baking powder, 1/2 teaspoon of baking soda, and 1/4 teaspoon of salt. Crack the 2 eggs and beat with a whisk in a cup. In a separate bowl, combine the 1-cup of buttermilk (low fat), 3/4 cup of skim milk, beaten eggs, and the tablespoon of honey. Gradually add the dry ingredients, do not over stir.

Next, place the diced apples in a microwave safe dish, cover with plastic wrap, and microwave on normal for 2 minutes to soften.

Turn the heat to medium on a non-stick skillet or griddle. Ladle out about a fourth a cup of batter onto the hot surface. Spoon a couple of apples over the top, flip after a couple of minutes. Repeat until all the batter and apples are gone. Drizzle with the maple syrup or your favorite syrup over the top, or sprinkle cinnamon and sugar over the top.

Zucchini Frittata

This delicious breakfast would make a good dinner choice too, as it's healthy and filling, full of feta cheese, zucchini, potatoes and turkey bacon. Makes 4 servings.

What You'll Need:

4 eggs + 2 egg whites
2 strips of turkey bacon (cooked, crumbled)
1 zucchini (grated and dried with a towel)
1 cup of potatoes (russet, cubed)
1/2 cup of feta cheese
1/2 cup of onion (chopped fine)
2 tablespoons of cilantro (fresh chopped)
1 tablespoon of olive oil
3/4 teaspoon of salt
1/2 teaspoon of garlic (minced)
1/4 teaspoon of hot sauce

How to Make It:

Add the 1 cup of cubed potatoes to a saucepan and cover with water, bring to a boil on high heat, then turn down to medium high. Cook for about 7 minutes or until the potatoes are tender enough to eat. Remove from heat, drain the water and place in a bowl. Using a paper towel, dry the potato cubes.

In a bowl, add the 4 eggs and 2 egg whites and beat with a whisk. Stir in the cup of cilantro, 3/4 teaspoon of salt, and 1/4 teaspoon of hot sauce.

Turn the on the oven broiler to high.

Place an ovenproof skillet on the stove (about a 10 inch size) and turn to medium high heat. Add the tablespoon of olive oil and sauté the 1/2 cup of fine chopped onion and the 1/2 teaspoon of minced garlic. Stir in the grated zucchini and cook for another 5 minutes. Stir in the cooked potato cubes, browning them for about 4 minutes. Next, pour the whisked egg mixture over the potatoes and zucchini. Place the skillet back on medium heat, lifting the edges to allow the egg to run, for a couple of minutes. Next, sprinkle the 2 strips of crumbled turkey bacon and the 1/2 cup of feta cheese over the top and place under the broiler for 5 minutes. Serve hot.

Intermittent Fasting Diet Dinner Recipes

Balsamic Turkey Meatloaf

If you are a meatloaf lover you will enjoy this different twist for meatloaf, which is a bit healthier than the beef counterpart. Makes 8 servings.

What You'll Need:

1.5 pounds of ground turkey
1 zucchini (fine diced)
1 bell pepper (red fine diced)
1 bell pepper (yellow fine diced)
1 egg
1 cup of bread crumbs
3/4 cup of ketchup (divided)
1/4 cup + 2 tablespoons of balsamic vinegar
1/4 cup of Parmesan cheese (grated)
1/4 cup of Romano cheese (grated)
1/4 cup of parsley (fresh chopped)
2 tablespoons of olive oil (extra-virgin)
1 tablespoon of thyme (fresh fine chopped)
2 1/2 teaspoons of garlic (minced)
1/2 teaspoon of red pepper flakes
Salt and pepper

How to Make It:

Prep: Preheat oven to 425 degrees Fahrenheit. Line a 9x5 inch loaf pan with foil.

Add the 2 tablespoons of extra virgin olive oil to a skillet on high heat and sauté the fine diced zucchini, red and yellow bell peppers, 2 1/2 teaspoons of minced garlic and dashes of salt and pepper for about 5 minutes. Set aside.

Crack the egg in a bowl and beat with a whisk, and stir in the 1/4 cup of fresh chopped parsley and the tablespoon of fresh fine chopped thyme. Add the 1.5 pounds of ground turkey, breaking it up with your hands, along with the cup of breadcrumbs, 1/4 cup of grated Parmesan cheese, 1/4 cup of grated Romano cheese, 1/2 cup of ketchup, 2 tablespoons of balsamic vinegar, and the zucchini and bell peppers. Mix with bare hands and mold into a loaf. Add to the lined loaf pan. Make the sauce for the topping by mixing the 1/4 cup of ketchup with the 1/4 cup of balsamic vinegar and the 1/2 teaspoon of red pepper flakes, and dashes of salt and pepper. Stir with a whisk, and then pour over the top of the meat loaf. Cook for 1 hour and 15 minutes, until the internal temperature of the meatloaf reaches 165 degrees Fahrenheit with a meat thermometer.

Buffalo Chicken with Slaw

Buffalo chicken is always associated as an appetizer but here it is a delicious main meal with a side of fresh homemade slaw. Makes 4 servings.

What You'll Need:

4 chicken breast halves (boneless, skinless, cut into strips)
4 cups of cabbage (shredded)
2 cups of buttermilk
2 cups of carrots (grated)
2 cups of bread crumbs (fine)
1 cup of celery (thin sliced)
1/2 cup of canola oil
1/2 cup of mayonnaise
1/2 cup of sour cream
1/2 cup of blue cheese (crumbles)
2 tablespoons of hot sauce (divided)
Salt and pepper

How to Make It:

Combine the 2 cups of buttermilk with 1 tablespoon of hot sauce and dashes of salt and pepper. Put the 4 boneless, skinless chicken breast halves cut into strips into a shallow dish. Pour the buttermilk mixture over the chicken, cover and refrigerate for 60 minutes. Combine the 1/2 cup of mayonnaise with the 1/2 cup of sour cream and the 1/2 cup of blue cheese crumbles in a blender or food processor until nice and lump free (this is the dressing). Using a whisk, add the remaining tablespoon of hot sauce and mix. In a bowl, add the 4 cups of shredded cabbage, 2 cups of grated carrots, with the 1 cup of thin sliced celery and toss. Pour 3/4 cup of the dressing over the cabbage mixture and toss to coat all. There will be 1/4 cup of dressing left over for a dipping sauce.

Add the 2 cups of fine bread crumbs to a shallow dish. Shake each chicken strip from the marinade and roll in the bread crumbs. Pour the 1/2 cup of canola oil into a skillet and turn to medium high heat. Fry each coated chicken strip for 4 minutes, turn and cook another 4 minutes, until all the chicken is cooked.

Serve with a side of slaw and dip in the dressing.

Edamame and Grilled Salmon

It is hard to beat salmon in terms of nutrition and flavor. This delicious meal is savory to the palate the filling. Makes 4 servings.

What You'll Need:

4 salmon fillets (skin on)
2 scallions (fine chopped)
1 1/3 cup of Edamame (cooked)
1/4 cup of cilantro leaves (fresh fine chopped)
2 teaspoons of canola oil
2 teaspoons of lime juice
2 teaspoons of soy sauce
2 teaspoons of honey
1 teaspoon of ginger (grated)
1/4 teaspoon of sesame seeds (black)
Salt and pepper
lime wedges (for garnish)

How to Make It:

Prep: Preheat the grill to medium high. Rub canola oil on the grates.

Mix the 2 fine chopped scallions with the 1/4 cup of

fresh fine chopped cilantro leaves, 2 teaspoons of canola oil, and the teaspoon of grated ginger. Dash salt and pepper and toss. Cut into the middle of the skins of the salmon fillets, making 2 slits about three inches in length from top to bottom, cutting halfway into the salmon. Do so with each fillet, and evenly spoon the scallions and cilantro into each slit. Salt and pepper the rest of the salmon fillets. In a cup, mix the 2 teaspoons of lime juice, 2 teaspoons of soy sauce, with the 2 teaspoons of honey with a whisk. Gently set each salmon fillet on the grill with the skin / herbs side facing up. Grill for about 3 1/2 minutes. Flip the salmon, brush the top with the lime juice sauce mixture and grill for another 3 1/2 minutes. Place cooked salmon fillets on a serving platter; evenly sprinkle the 1/4 teaspoon of black sesame seeds over the tops. Garnish with the lime wedges and serve with the 1 1/3 cup of cooked Edamame in a serving dish.

Grilled Chicken Tostadas

This is a healthy meal made with tasty seasoned chicken breasts and a variety of other savory flavors. Makes 4 servings.

What You'll Need:

4 tortillas (flour, 8 inch)
2 chicken breasts (boneless, skinless, cut into bite-sized pieces)
1 pound of tomatillos (husked and rinsed)
4 lime wedges
1 chipotle chili in adobo sauce (chopped coarse)
2 cups of romaine lettuce (shredded)
1/3 cup of feta cheese (crumbled)
1/4 cup of lime juice
4 tablespoons of onions (fine chopped)
2 tablespoons of cilantro (fresh chopped)
1 tablespoon of olive oil
1 teaspoon of garlic (minced)
Salt

How to Make It:

In a large bowl, combine the 1/4 cup of lime juice with the coarse chopped chipotle chili in adobo sauce and dashes of salt. Toss in the 2 cut up boneless, skinless chicken breasts and cover. Refrigerate for 2 hours to marinate. Place the chicken pieces on greased skewers. Turn the grill to medium heat. Spray the 4 8-inch flour tortillas with cooking spray and grill them for about 45 seconds, flip and grill another 45 seconds. Place the skewered chicken and the pound of husked, rinsed tomatillos on the grill and turn every 30 seconds for about 5 minutes. Remove the chicken and tomatillos from the heat. Remove the skewers from the chicken. Chop the grilled tomatillos into bite sized chunks in a bowl. Add the tablespoon of olive oil and a dash of salt and toss. Layer the tostadas by placing a tortilla down first, then divide the 2 cups of shredded romaine lettuce, tomatillos, chicken, 4 tablespoons of onions (fine chopped), and the 2 tablespoons of cilantro (fresh chopped). Garnish each plate with a lime wedge. Enjoy.

Italian Chicken

This savory Italian Chicken dish goes well with a salad or steamed vegetables. Makes 6 servings.

What You'll Need:

4 chicken breast halves (bone- in, skinless)
2 chicken thighs (skinless, bone-in)
1 can of tomatoes (diced, 15 oz)
3 oz of prosciutto (chopped)
1/2 cup of white grape juice
1/2 cup of chicken stock
1/2 cup of bell pepper (red, sliced)
1/2 cup of bell pepper (yellow, sliced)
1/4 cup of olive oil
1/4 cup of parsley (fresh flat leaf, chopped)
2 tablespoons of capers
1 tablespoon of thyme (fresh)
1 1/2 teaspoon of salt (divided)
1 teaspoon of oregano (fresh)
1 teaspoon of garlic (minced)
1/2 teaspoon of pepper

How to Make It:

Rinse and pat dry the chicken. Rub 1/2 teaspoons each

of salt and pepper on all of the chicken. Pour the 1/4 cup of olive oil in a skillet and turn to medium heat. Add the chicken to the hot oil and brown on each side. Place on a platter and set to the side. In the same skillet add the 1/2 cups of chopped yellow and red bell peppers and the 3 oz of chopped prosciutto and sauté. Stir in the teaspoon of minced garlic and cook for another 60 seconds. Add the 15 oz can of diced tomatoes, 1/2 cup of white grape juice, 1 tablespoon of thyme (fresh), 1 1/2 teaspoon of salt (divided), 1 teaspoon of oregano (fresh), and 1 teaspoon of garlic (minced). Deglaze the skillet by scraping the bits from the bottom into the mixture. Add the cooked chicken and pout in the 1/2 cup of chicken stock. Turn the heat to high and bring to a boil. Cover, reduce the heat to low and simmer for about 25 minutes. When cooked, stir in the 1/4 cup of fresh chopped flat leaf parsley and the 2 tablespoons of capers, then serve.

Oriental Turkey Burgers

Here is a different twist to an American favorite, turkey burgers seasoned up with oriental spices. Makes 4 burgers.

What You'll Need:

12 oz of ground turkey
4 hamburger buns (whole grain)
2 scallions (chopped)
1/2 cup of water (boiling)
1/2 cup of English cucumber (sliced thin)
1/4 cup of balsamic vinegar
1/4 cup of bulgur wheat
1/4 cup of yogurt (plain)
1/4 cup of cilantro (fresh whole)
1/8 cup of onion (sliced thin)
2 tablespoons of hoisin sauce
2 tablespoons of cilantro (fresh chopped)
2 teaspoons of canola oil
1 teaspoon of sugar (granulated)
1 teaspoon of ginger (grated)
1 teaspoon of chili garlic sauce
1/2 teaspoon of garlic (minced)
Salt and pepper

How to Make It:

First, combine the 1/2 cup of boiling water with the 1/4 cup of bulgur wheat in a small bowl. Seal with plastic wrap and set aside for about 50 minutes. Next, using a whisk in a separate bowl mix the 1/4 cup of balsamic vinegar with the teaspoon of granulated sugar. Toss in the 1/2 cup of thin sliced English cucumber and the 1/8 cup of thin sliced onions. Sprinkle with dashes of salt and pepper. Cover and set in refrigerator for half an hour. In another bowl, whisk together the 1/4 cup of plain yogurt with the teaspoon of chili garlic sauce and more dashes of salt and pepper. Set the bowl aside while preparing the turkey. When the bulgur wheat is ready, drain the water and add the 12 oz of ground turkey, 2 chopped scallions, 2 tablespoons of hoisin sauce, 2 tablespoons of fresh chopped cilantro, teaspoon of grated ginger, and the 1/2 teaspoon of minced garlic. Mix with bare hands to insure good mixture. Separate into 4 patties. Add the 2 teaspoons of canola oil to a skillet and heat to medium high. Cook the turkey burgers until well done, 4 minutes on each side. Next, pour the cucumber mixture into a colander to drain, and then toss in the 1/4 cup of fresh whole cilantro leaves. Create the burgers by spreading the yogurt sauce onto each bun half, add the turkey burger, and then add a spoon of the cucumber cilantro mixture.

Enjoy.

Shepherd's Pie

This is a delicious and hearty one-dish meal. Makes 8 servings.

What You'll Need:

2 lbs. of potatoes (russet, scrubbed, peeled, chunked)
1.5 lbs. of ground beef (lean)
2 zucchinis (julienned)
8 oz. of mushrooms (button, sliced)
1 cup of carrots (peeled, grated)
1 cup of purple grape juice
1/2 cup of heavy cream
1/2 cup of bell pepper (red, julienned)
1/2 cup of Monterey Jack cheese (grated)
2 1/2 cup of beef stock (divided)
1/3 cup of butter
3/4 cup of onion (fine chopped, divided)
5 tablespoons of canola oil (divided)
3 tablespoons of flour (all-purpose)
2 tablespoons of tomato paste
2 teaspoons of Worcestershire sauce
1 teaspoon of paprika
1/2 teaspoon of cayenne pepper
1/2 teaspoon of garlic (minced)
Salt and pepper

Water

How to Make It:

Prep: Preheat the oven to 375 degrees Fahrenheit.

Add the 2 lbs. of scrubbed, peeled, chunked russet potatoes and the 1/2 teaspoon of minced garlic to a medium size saucepan and cover with water about an inch over the top of the potatoes. Dash some salt in the water and stir, turn heat to high and bring to a boil. Turn to medium high for about 15 minutes or until the potatoes are tender. Pour into a strainer to drain the water and return the potatoes to the saucepan. Add the 1/2 cup of heavy cream and the 3 tablespoons of butter and mash. Stir in dashes of salt and pepper and put aside.

In a large skillet add another tablespoon of butter with a tablespoon of canola oil and turn to medium high. Fry the 1.5 pounds of lean ground beef in the grease and add the 2 teaspoons of Worcestershire sauce and the 1/2 teaspoon of cayenne pepper and stir until the beef is well done. Season with dashes of salt and pepper. Add the 2 tablespoons of tomato sauce and stir over the heat. Pour in the 1/2 cup of beef stock and simmer for a few minutes. Pour the beef mixture in a large bowl and set aside. Add the remaining butter to the skillet and add 1/4 cup of fine chopped onions and sauté. Next add the 2 zucchinis (julienned), 1 cup of carrots (peeled, grated), 1/2 cup of bell pepper (red, julienned) and the teaspoon of paprika and stir. Cook an additional 10 minutes. Take off heat.

Create the pie by layering with 1/2 of the beef into the bottom of a 9x12 inch baking dish. Sprinkle the 1/2 cup of grated Monterey Jack cheese over the beef layer; add the remainder of the beef, pressing down firmly with a spoon back. Next, layer with the sautéed vegetables, and then add the mashed potatoes on top. Season the top with paprika and place in the oven to bake until the edges turn a golden brown, about 30 minutes.

While the pie is baking, make the gravy by pouring 3 tablespoons of canola oil into a saucepan and sautéing 1/4 cup of chopped onions and the 8 oz of sliced button mushrooms, until they are soft. Stir in the 3 tablespoons of all-purpose flour and using a whisk pour in the 2 cups of beef stock and the cup of purple grape juice and stir until it thickens. Season with salt and pepper as desired. Pour over slices of shepherd's pie and enjoy.

Shrimp Scampi

If you love shrimp, you will love this recipe, complete with whole grain noodles. Makes 4 servings.

What You'll Need:

16 shrimp (large, deveined, shelled)
6 oz of spaghetti noodles (whole grain)
6 black olives (pitted, chopped)
1/2 cup of onions (sliced thin)
1/4 cup of croutons (multi-grain, crumbed)
1/4 cup of parsley (fresh flat leaf, divided)
1/4 cup of chicken stock
1/4 cup of white grape juice
1 1/2 tablespoons of lemon zest (divided)
1 tablespoon of lemon juice
1 tablespoon of olive oil
1/2 teaspoon of garlic (minced)
1/4 teaspoon of red pepper flakes (crushed)
1/4 teaspoon of salt

How to Make It:

Cook the spaghetti noodles according to the directions on the package to "al dente." In a separate bowl, add the 1/4 cup of croutons (multi-grain, crumbed),

1/2 tablespoon of parsley (fresh flat leaf), and a tablespoon of the lemon zest and stir, let sit. Meanwhile, in a skillet, add the tablespoon of olive oil and turn to medium heat. Stir in the 1/2 cup of thin sliced onions, 1/2 teaspoon of garlic (minced), 1/4 teaspoon of red pepper flakes (crushed) and sauté for a minute. Stir in the 16 large deveined and shelled shrimp and the 1/4 teaspoon of salt and cook for another 90 seconds. Add the 1/4 cup of chicken stock, 1/4 cup of white grape juice, tablespoon of lemon juice and the 6 chopped, pitted black olives. Turn heat to high and bring to a boil, stirring and cooking for a minutes, then turn the heat back down to medium. Add the cook spaghetti noodles and the remainder of the parsley and lemon zest. Toss and pour into a serving dish. Sprinkle the 1/4 cup of crumbles multi-grain croutons over the top and serve.

Vegetable Pot Pie

Sometimes you simply do not need meat to make a full meal. This is a perfect tasty pot pie and all the better because it's homemade. Makes 8 servings.

What You'll Need:

2 pie crusts (9-inch deep dish, unbaked, rolled)
1 3/4 cup of vegetable stock
1 cup of carrots (thin sliced)
1 cup of English peas (frozen)
1 cup of potatoes (diced)
2/3 cup of milk
1/2 cup of celery (thin sliced)
1/2 cup of butter
1/3 cup of onion (fine chopped)
1/3 cup of flour (all-purpose, unbleached)
Salt and pepper
1/4 teaspoon of celery seed
1/4 teaspoon of garlic powder
Water

How to Make It:

Prep: Preheat the oven to 425 degrees Fahrenheit.

Place a saucepan over high heat and add 1 cup of carrots (thin sliced), 1 cup of English peas (frozen), 1 cup of potatoes (diced), and 1/2 cup of celery (thin sliced) and add enough water to cover the vegetables and bring the water to a boil. Add a lid and cook for 15 minutes, vegetables are done when they are tender. Drain water and set aside for a few minutes. Place a skillet on medium heat and add the 1/2 cup of butter and sauté the 1/3 cup of fine chopped onions. Add the 1/3 cup of flour (all-purpose, unbleached), dashes of salt and pepper, 1/4 teaspoon of celery seed, and 1/4 teaspoon of garlic powder and stir. Cook until well blended for a couple of minutes. Combine with the 1 3/4 cup of vegetable stock and the 2/3 cup of milk. Turn the heat to medium low and simmer for 5 more minutes. Turn off heat and stir in the cooked vegetables. Unroll a pie crust and place in a 9 inch deep dish pie pan. Add the vegetable mixture into the pie crust. Unroll the other pie crust and carefully place on top of the vegetable pie, sealing the edges but pressing a fork to make small ridges. Cut a couple of slits in the crust to vent the steam while cooking. Place on a baking sheet and in the oven for 35 minutes. Allow to sit to cool for about 10 minutes before serving.

Intermittent Fasting Diet Light Snack Recipes

Apple and Turkey Ham Salad

This is a delightfully crunchy sweet and savory salad. Makes 6 servings.

What You'll Need:

1/2 pound of turkey ham (thin sliced, torn)
4 endives (crosswise sliced)
3 apples (crisp, cored, sliced thin)
2 bunches of trimmed watercress
2 cups of onions (sliced thin)
1/4 cup of sour cream
1/4 cup of water
3 tablespoons of olive oil (extra virgin)
2 tablespoons of lemon juice
2 tablespoons of apple cider vinegar
2 tablespoons of Dijon mustard
Salt and pepper

How to Make It:

Add the 3 thin sliced apples into a bowl, pour over the 2 tablespoons of lemon juice, and toss to coat. Add the 3 tablespoons of extra virgin olive oil to a skillet on medium heat. Stir in the 2 cups of thin sliced onions and dashes of salt and sauté. Add the 2 tablespoons of apple cider vinegar and the 2 tablespoons of Dijon mustard in with the onions and stir with a whisk. Add the 1/4 cups of sour cream and water and continue stirring with the whisk. Pour the dressing over the lemon apples and toss. Toss in the 4 crosswise sliced endives, 2 bunches of trimmed watercress and the 1/2 pound of thin sliced and torn turkey ham. Add dashes of salt and pepper and toss before serving.

Baked Potatoes Twice

Baked potatoes are a tasty light meal, but "twice" baked potatoes are even better! Makes 4 servings.

What You'll Need:

4 potatoes (medium sized russet works best)
1/2 cup of onions (thin sliced)
1/2 cup of cream cheese with chives
1/2 cup of milk
1 tablespoon of butter
1 tablespoon of parsley (fresh chopped, plus 4 pinches)
2 teaspoons of thyme (fresh chopped)
1 teaspoon of canola oil
1 teaspoon of garlic (minced)
Salt and pepper

How to Make It:

Prep: Preheat the oven to 375 degrees Fahrenheit. Wash the potatoes, pat dry, and then rub the outside with the teaspoon of canola oil. Sprinkle salt over them and place in the oven, with a baking sheet on the rack below. Bake for 75 minutes; remove from the oven to cool.

Add the tablespoon of butter to a skillet on medium heat. Stir in the 1/2 cup of thin sliced onions and dashes of salt and pepper for about 7 minutes. Stir in the 2 teaspoons of fresh chopped thyme and the teaspoon of minced garlic, stirring for a minute. Remove from heat. Cut the potatoes in half, lengthwise, leaving the skin intact on the bottom. Carefully scoop the meat of the potato, leaving the skins intact. Place the scooped potatoes into the onion mixture and mix. Combine with the 1/2 cup of cream cheese with chives and the 1/2 cup of milk, the potatoes will be lumpy. Add the tablespoon of fresh chopped parsley and mix well. Evenly spoon the potato mixture back into the potato skins. Place the potato halves on the baking sheet and return to the hot oven for about 23 minutes. Garnish with a pinch of fresh chopped parsley and enjoy.

Broccoli Cheese Soup

Here is a lighter meal, made with wholesome broccoli, savory herbs, and delicious cheese. Makes 4 servings.

What You'll Need:

1 package of broccoli florets (frozen, 16 oz)
3 cups of chicken stock
1 1/4 cups of Cheddar cheese (shredded, sharp)
1 cup of French bread (large cubes)
1 cup of onions (sliced)
1/2 cup of heavy cream
5 tablespoons of butter (divided)
3 tablespoons of flour (all-purpose)
2 tablespoons of olive oil (extra virgin)
1/2 teaspoon of garlic (minced)
1/2 teaspoon of thyme (fresh chopped)
1/4 teaspoon of white pepper (ground)
1/4 teaspoon of Creole seasoning
Salt
Nutmeg

How to Make It:

Add 3 tablespoons of butter to a medium saucepan turn to medium high heat. Sauté the 1 cup of sliced onions and add dashes of salt, nutmeg, and 1/4 teaspoon of ground white pepper. Stir in the 1/2 teaspoon of minced garlic and the 1/2 teaspoon of fresh chopped thyme for several seconds. While stirring with a whisk, sprinkle in the 3 tablespoons of all-purpose flour, keep stirring for about 2 minutes over the heat. Pour in the 3 cups of chicken stock, continue to stir with the whisk until all the lumps are gone. Turn the heat to high to bring to a boil while stirring. Turn the heat to low and simmer for 5 minutes, stirring often. Add the 16 oz package of frozen broccoli florets and cook for another 10 minutes, stirring often. If desired, pour into a blender and food processor to blend. Or stir with a masher, mashing the broccoli. Return to the saucepan on low heat. Preheat the oven to 400 degrees Fahrenheit. Pour in the 1/2 cup of heavy cream, stirring while the cream heats. Pour in the 1 1/4 cups of Cheddar cheese, stirring until melted. Add the last 2 tablespoons of butter, stirring until melted and blended.

Put the 1 cup of large cubed French bread and toss with the 2 tablespoons of extra virgin olive oil and the 1/4 teaspoon of Creole seasoning. Spread on a baking sheet and bake for 3 minutes in the hot oven. Remove to flip the croutons over and bake another 3 minutes.

Ladle soup and top with the croutons to serve.

Cauliflower Soup

Here is a delicious and filling, yet light, soup. Makes 4 servings.

What You'll Need:

1 head of cauliflower (chopped florets)
4 parsley leaves (fresh)
6 cups of chicken stock
1 cup of potatoes (scrubbed, skin-on, cubed)
1/2 cup of milk
1/2 cup of onions (chopped)
1 tablespoon of canola oil
1 teaspoon of butter
Salt and pepper

How to Make It:

Add the tablespoon of canola oil and the teaspoon of butter to a large saucepan over medium low heat. Stir in the 1/2 cup of chopped onions, cook and stir for 10 minutes. Add the heat of chopped cauliflower florets, 6 cups of chicken stock, and the cup of cubed potatoes and season with dashes of salt and pepper. Turn the heat to high and bring liquid to a boil. Turn heat to medium, cover and cook for 20 more minutes, until the vegetables are tender. Pour the soup into a blender or food processor to combine until smooth. Pour back into the saucepan and reheat to medium. Add more salt and pepper to taste. Thick soup may be thinned with extra milk. Garnish with a fresh parsley leaf in each bowl.

Greens with Baked Beans

This is a delicious one dish meal that offers wholesome beans along with smoked turkey ham and savory herbs. Makes 6 servings.

What You'll Need:

1 bunch of greens (mustard greens or Swiss chard, chopped, stems removed)
2 cans of pinto beans (drained, rinsed, 15 oz)
1 can of navy beans (undrained, 15oz)
1 can of tomatoes (crushed 15 oz)
1/2 cup of smoked turkey ham (diced)
1/2 cup of celery (fine chopped)
1/2 cup of carrots (fine chopped)
1/4 cup of parsley (fresh chopped)
1/4 cup of onion (chopped)
1/4 cup of water
1 tablespoon of olive oil (extra virgin)
1 teaspoon of garlic (minced)
1 teaspoon of thyme (fresh chopped)
1 teaspoon of oregano (fresh chopped)
Salt and pepper

How to Make It:

Prep: Preheat oven to 375 degrees Fahrenheit. Place a large skillet on the stove on medium heat and add the tablespoon of olive oil. Stir in and sauté the 1/2 cup of celery (fine chopped), 1/2 cup of carrots (fine chopped), 1/4 cup of onion (chopped), and 1 teaspoon of garlic (minced). Season with salt and pepper. Stir in the bunch of greens along with the 1/2 cup of diced smoked turkey ham and 1/4 cup of water. Cook for 3 minutes. Stir in the can of crushed tomatoes and turn the heat to medium high for 5 minutes. Stir in the 2 cans of drained, rinsed pinto beans, and the can of undrained navy beans. Next add the 1/4 cup of parsley (fresh chopped), 1 teaspoon of thyme (fresh chopped), and the 1 teaspoon of oregano (fresh chopped). Stir and heat through. Using a potato masher, mash the some of the beans (not all). Sprinkle with salt and pepper. Pour into a baking dish (2 quart) and cover with foil. Bake for 55 minutes, removing the foil for the last 10. Allow to cool for about 5 minutes before serving.

Maple Flavored Sweet Potato Fries

Here is a healthy and sweet version of a favorite, a nice alternative to French fries. Makes 6 servings.

What You'll Need:

5 sweet potatoes (peeled and cut into small wedges)
1 tablespoon of canola oil
1 tablespoon of maple syrup
1/2 teaspoon of lemon zest
Salt and pepper
Nutmeg

How to Make It:

Prep: Preheat the oven to 425 degrees Fahrenheit. Line a baking sheet with foil.

Place the sweet potato wedges in a large bowl, add the tablespoon of canola oil, and toss to coach each piece. Add dashes of salt and pepper. Place the wedges on the foil lined baking sheet and place in the hot oven for 20 minutes. Take the baking sheet out of the oven and place the wedges back in the bowl. This time add the tablespoon of maple syrup and toss to coat all. Place the potatoes back on the baking sheet and bake for 7 minutes, then flip the potato wedges and bake another 7 minutes. Add to a serving bowl, toss with the 1/2 teaspoon of lemon zest and dashes of salt, pepper, and nutmeg before serving.

Nutty Cucumber Mango Rice Salad

Enjoy something different made with peanuts, mangos, cucumbers and rice. Makes 6 servings.

What You'll Need:

2 scallions (sliced thin)
1 cucumber (English, diced)
1 jalapeno (red, seeded, diced)
1 1/2 cups of saffron rice
1 cup of mango (chopped)
1/2 cup of cilantro (fresh chopped)
1/3 cup of peanuts (salted, roasted, chopped)
1/4 cup of quinoa (rinsed)
2 tablespoons of lime juice
2 tablespoons of canola oil
1 tablespoon of lime zest
1 teaspoon of sugar (granulated)
Salt and pepper
Water

How to Make It:

Cook the 1 1/2 cups of saffron rice according to the package directions. In another saucepan add water and dashes of water and turn heat to high to bring to a boil.

Stir in the 1/4 cup of rinsed quinoa and turn heat to medium high. Cook for 12 minutes, until it turns tender. Pour into a colander and rinse with cool water and drain. In a separate bowl, combine the 2 tablespoons of lime juice, 2 tablespoons of canola oil, tablespoon of lime zest, teaspoon of granulated sugar and dashes of salt and pepper, using a whisk. Stir in the cook saffron rice, 2 thin sliced scallions, diced English cucumber, seeded and diced red jalapeno, cup of chopped mango, 1/2 cup of fresh chopped cilantro 1/3 cup of salted, roasted, chopped peanuts, and the cooked quinoa. Toss and season with more salt and pepper if desired.

Open Face Tomato and Mozzarella Herb Sandwich

This is a unique twist from a sandwich; there is no meat, just the delicious tomato and smoked Mozzarella with savory herbs on a baguette roll. Makes 4 servings.

What You'll Need:

4 slices of smoked mozzarella (thick)
4 slices of tomato (thick)
1 demi baguette (4 oz.)
2 tablespoons of parsley (fresh chopped)
1 1/2 tablespoons of Parmesan cheese (fine grated)
2 teaspoons of thyme (fresh chopped)
2 teaspoons of olive oil
1 teaspoon of garlic (minced)
Salt and pepper

How to Make It:

Prep: Preheat the oven to broil.

In a bowl, add the 2 tablespoons of fresh chopped parsley, 2 teaspoons of fresh chopped thyme, teaspoon of minced garlic and 2 teaspoons of olive oil and combine. Slice the baguette lengthwise in two. Cut in half so you have 4 pieces of bread. Evenly divide and spread the herbs over the bread, face up. Evenly sprinkle the 1 1/2 tablespoons of fine grated Parmesan cheese over the 4 slices. Bake under the broiler for 2 minutes. Remove and add a slice of tomato, and a slice of smoked mozzarella cheese on top of each slice of bread. Return to the broiler long enough for the cheese to melt, about a minute or two. Serve hot.

Orange Stir Fry Vegetables

This is a light dish made with just vegetables with the light fruity flavor of orange. Makes 4 servings.

What You'll Need:

1 can of water chestnuts (drained, 4oz)
1 cup of orange juice
1 cup of celery (chopped)
1 cup of mushrooms (rinsed, sliced)
1/2 cup of bell pepper (red, thin sliced)
1/2 cup of carrots (sliced)
1/2 cup of squash (sliced yellow)
1/2 cup of broccoli (chopped)
1/4 cup of baby corn
1/4 cup of snow peas
1/8 cup of onions (thin sliced)
2 tablespoons of cornstarch
2 tablespoons of orange zest
2 tablespoons of canola oil (divided)
1 tablespoon of soy sauce
1 teaspoon of ginger (chopped)
1 teaspoon of garlic (minced)
Salt
4 orange slices
Cooked rice (enough for 4 servings)

How to Make It:

Pour the cup of orange juice into a bowl and combine with the 2 tablespoons of cornstarch, tablespoon of soy sauce, teaspoon of chopped ginger, teaspoon of minced garlic and dashes of salt. Add a wok or large skillet to high heat and pour in the tablespoon of canola oil and sauté the cup of sliced mushrooms, 1/2 cup of sliced carrots, and the 1/8 cup of thin sliced onions for just one minute. Mix in the 1/2 cup of sliced yellow squash, 1/2 cup of chopped broccoli, and 1/4 cup of snow peas. Stir in the 4 oz can of drained water chestnuts, cup of chopped celery, 1/2 cup of thin sliced red bell peppers, and 1/4 cup of baby corn. Cook for another couple of minutes. Pour in the orange sauce, stir and heat through. Serve over the cooked rice and garnish with the 2 tablespoons of orange zest and an orange slice on each plate.

Parsley Mint Roasted Carrots

This is a delicious way to eat your carrots, and nutritious to boot. Makes 4 servings.

What You'll Need:

2 1/2 cups of carrots (halved lengthwise and cut into 2-inch chunks)
1/2 cup of chicken stock
1/4 cup of mint (fresh chopped)
1/4 cup of parsley (fresh chopped)
4 teaspoons of olive oil
2 teaspoons of lemon juice
1/2 teaspoon of lemon zest
Salt and pepper

How to Make It:

Pour the 1/2 cup of chicken broth in a skillet and turn to medium high heat. Add the 2/12 cups of chunked carrots and a teaspoon of olive oil, stir, and bring to a boil. Place a lid on, reduce heat to medium, and cook for 13 more minutes. Remove the lid, stir and cook off all of the chicken stock and cook the carrots another 3 minutes to slight brown. Add dashes of salt and pepper. In a small bowl mix the 1/4 cup of fresh chopped mint,

1/4 cup of fresh chopped parsley, 2 teaspoons of lemon juice and 1/2 teaspoon of lemon zest. Place the carrots in a serving bowl and toss with the mint, parsley mixture. Serve warm.

Quinoa with Herbs

Quinoa is a super food because of the high levels of nutrients within it. Makes 4 servings.

What You'll Need:

2 3/4 cups of chicken stock
1 1/2 cups of quinoa
3/4 cup of basil (fresh chopped leaves)
1/4 cup of parsley (fresh chopped)
1/2 cup of lemon juice (divided)
1/4 cup of olive oil (extra virgin)
1 tablespoon of thyme (fresh chopped leaves)
2 teaspoons of lemon zest
Salt and pepper

How to Make It:

Pour the 2 3/4 cups of chicken stock into a medium size saucepan along with the 1 1/2 cups of quinoa and the 1/4 cup of lemon juice, turn to medium high heat, and bring to a boil. Place lid on saucepan, turn to low, and simmer for about 14 minutes. Meanwhile, combine the 3/4 cup of basil (fresh chopped leaves), 1/4 cup of parsley (fresh chopped), 1/4 cup of lemon juice (divided), 1/4 cup of olive oil (extra virgin), 1 tablespoon of thyme (fresh chopped leaves), 2 teaspoons of lemon zest, and dashes of salt and pepper in a small bowl. When the quinoa is cooked, add to a serving bowl and pour the "dressing" over, tossing to coat all. Add extra salt and pepper if desired.

Spicy Tomatoes and Green Beans

Sometimes you just need a pick-me-up and this dish will do it with the light flavor of cinnamon with tomatoes and green beans. Makes 6 servings.

What You'll Need:

4 cups of green beans (trimmed)
1 can of tomatoes (15 oz crushed)
1 1/4 cups of water
1/4 cup of onions (chopped)
3 tablespoons of olive oil
Salt and pepper
Cinnamon

How to Make It:

Add the 3 tablespoons to a skillet and sauté the 1/4 cup of onions. In a medium saucepan, add the 4 cups of green beans (trimmed), 1 can of tomatoes (15 oz crushed), 1 1/4 cups of water, sautéed onions, and dashes of salt and pepper and cinnamon. Stir and bring the water to a boil over high heat. Turn to medium low and simmer partial cover with a lid on for 35 minutes or until the green beans is tender. Season with more salt and pepper if desired.

Spinach Salad with Pomegranate Dressing

Spinach salad is a delicious meal made with pomegranate juice and walnuts, guaranteed to delight the taste buds. Makes 4 servings.

What You'll Need:

4 cups of spinach (baby)
1 cup of mushrooms (white button, sliced thin)
3/4 cup of tomatoes (grape, halved)
1/2 cup of walnuts (chopped)
1/4 cup of onions (thin sliced)
1/4 cup of pomegranate juice (plus 2 tablespoons)
1 tablespoon of apple cider vinegar
1 tablespoon of olive oil (extra virgin)
1 teaspoon of sugar (granulated)
Salt and pepper
Water and ice

How to Make It:

Pour 1/4 cup of pomegranate juice into a skillet and add the teaspoon of granulated sugar and a couple of dashes of salt. Turn heat to medium high and simmer for several minutes, stir often. Stir in the 1/2 cup of chopped walnuts and cook for another 5 minutes, the liquid should evaporate. Pour the nuts onto a cool baking sheet break apart when cooled.

Place the 1/4 cup of thin sliced onions in a bowl and cover with ice and water for 10 minutes. Drain the water and dry the onions with a paper towel. Put the 4 cups of baby spinach in a salad bowl, and then layer the cold onions, followed by the cup of thin sliced white button mushrooms, 3/4 cup of halved grape tomatoes, and the walnuts. In a separate bowl, combine the 2 tablespoons of pomegranate juice with the tablespoon of apple cider vinegar, tablespoon of extra virgin olive oil, and dashes of salt and pepper, using a whisk. Pour the dressing over the spinach salad and toss, and then serve.

www.ingramcontent.com/pod-product-compliance
Ingram Content Group UK Ltd.
Pitfield, Milton Keynes, MK11 3LW, UK
UKHW020142250726
13967UKWH00002B/809

9 781633 830677